The Principal

J. C. Snaith

Alpha Editions

This edition published in 2024

ISBN 9789362511928

Design and Setting By
Alpha Editions
www.alphaedis.com
Email - info@alphaedis.com

As per information held with us this book is in Public Domain.
This book is a reproduction of an important historical work.
Alpha Editions uses the best technology to reproduce historical work
in the same manner it was first published to preserve its original nature.
Any marks or number seen are left intentionally to preserve.

Contents

CHAPTER I	- 1 -
CHAPTER II	- 4 -
CHAPTER III	- 7 -
CHAPTER IV	- 11 -
CHAPTER V	- 16 -
CHAPTER VI	- 27 -
CHAPTER VII	- 35 -
CHAPTER VIII	- 44 -
CHAPTER IX	- 48 -
CHAPTER X	- 58 -
CHAPTER XI	- 63 -
CHAPTER XII	- 67 -
CHAPTER XIII	- 71 -
CHAPTER XIV	- 77 -
CHAPTER XV	- 88 -
CHAPTER XVI	- 91 -
CHAPTER XVII	- 96 -
CHAPTER XVIII	- 101 -
CHAPTER XIX	- 107 -
CHAPTER XX	- 111 -
CHAPTER XXI	- 115 -
CHAPTER XXII	- 122 -
CHAPTER XXIII	- 131 -
CHAPTER XXIV	- 138 -

CHAPTER XXV	- 149 -
CHAPTER XXVI	- 154 -
CHAPTER XXVII	- 166 -
CHAPTER XXVIII	- 171 -

CHAPTER I
A GREAT PROCONSUL; AND OTHER PHENOMENA

THE great Proconsul stood on one of Messrs. Maple's best hearthrugs in Grosvenor Square. A typical payer of the super-tax, a pink and prosperous gentleman in a morning coat and striped trousers, his appearance had long commanded the admiration of his country.

He had not ruled the teeming millions of the Ganges, although the strength of his digestion and his absence of imagination would at any time have enabled him to do so. But for a period of nine weeks he had been the Resident of Barataria North-West; and partly for that reason and partly for a reason even more cogent, he had the distinction of being the last peer created by Mr. Vandeleur's last government.

The world is familiar with Sir William Richmond's fine portrait of Walter Augustus, first Baron Shelmerdine of Potterhanworth now, on loan at the National Portrait Gallery. In this the national asset appears as he encountered his Sovereign in knee breeches, silk stockings, shoe buckles and other regalia.

Competent judges consider it an excellent likeness, and of course quite unexceptionable as a work of art. It is the portrait of a happily endowed Englishman in his manly prime, to which the nation at large is able to refer between the hours of ten and four, Fridays excepted.

Eton, Balliol, diplomacy, private means, together with various places of emolument under the Crown, had each a share in raising Shelmerdine of Potterhanworth to his elevation. A first baron certainly, but not a mushroom growth. The honors of a grateful nation had come to him mainly because he had not been able to avoid them. From early youth he had been ranged with those who always do the right thing at the right time in the right way. He had always hit the bull's-eye so exactly in the centre that public regard had had to strive to keep pace with his progress.

Up till the age of one-and-thirty, Shelmerdine—not then of Potterhanworth—had like humbler mortals just a sporting chance of getting off the target. But at the age of thirty-one he married. By that judicious action he forfeited any little chance he may have had of dying an obscure, private individual.

Sociologists differ as to what is the most portentous phenomenon of the age in which we dwell, but there is a body of the well-informed which awards the palm unhesitatingly to that amiable institution, the Suffolk Colthurst.

The world is under great obligations to this interesting representative of the higher mammalia. The upper reaches of Theology are whitened with the bones of the Suffolk Colthurst. It makes an almost ideal Under-Secretary, it is always so smooth-spoken and well-brushed; it makes a most excellent Judge; there is no place of emolument it is not fitted to grace; and in the unlikely event of a doubt invading your mind as to whether the particular schoolmaster will be inducted to the vacant see of Wincanton, you have only to look up which branch it was of the Suffolk Colthursts into which he married, and at what period of his life he married her.

What would be the Established Order without the Colthurst of Suffolk? What would be the Navy and Army, Law and Medicine, Parliament itself, Art—and yes, gentlemen!—Letters, without the Colthurst of Suffolk?

It is an error, however, to suppose that this pleasant phenomenon confines itself to one little corner of the globe. The Colthurst is indigenous to Suffolk, but for generations there has been quite a colony settled in Kent. There is also the world-famous Scotch variety, and of late traces of the Suffolk Colthurst have been found in America. The Transatlantic mind, never slow at diagnosis, and with its trick of masterful and telling speech, has already ventured to define its creed. In America the creed of the Suffolk Colthurst has been defined as the Art of Getting There with Both Feet.

Please do not assume that there is anything ignoble about the Colthurst of Suffolk. Quite the contrary. It has been laid down as a general principle that the Suffolk Colthurst never makes money but always marries it. That is not to say, of course, that a Suffolk Colthurst has never been known to make money, because such a statement, however pleasant, would be in excess of the truth. But the Suffolk Colthurst, *pur sang*, sets less store by the making of money than by the spending of money in the way that shows it has always had money to spend.

As a matter of fact it always has had money to spend. As soon as banking, brewing, land-jobbing, share-broking, and other polite arts began to flourish in Suffolk, the Colthurst began to marry and to give in marriage. And to this day if you enter a small private bank in a quiet cathedral city, and you take the trouble to make inquiries, you are quite likely to learn that the local Suffolk Colthurst has the chief proprietary interest in the concern. The family has always been partial to banking. It is such an eminently sensible practice to lend money at double the rate at which you borrow it; and it has the additional advantage that you can't call it Trade.

Our immediate business, however, is with the blameless gentleman who at the age of one-and-thirty was accepted in marriage by a charming representative of the genus, and at the age of nine-and-fifty was made a peer by Mr. Vandeleur's government, immediately antecedent to its total and permanent eclipse.

To return, then, to Shelmerdine of Potterhanworth. For nearly an hour had he occupied the tasteful hearthrug provided by Messrs. Maple. A frown chequered his serene front and several times he had recourse to the Leading Morning Journal which lay open on his writing-table at page four.

At the top of the third column was a communication dated from the Helicon Club, S. W. It was signed by himself and had been crowned with the glory of the largest type you could have without having to pay for it. Immediately below, in type equally glorious, were communications veiled in the discreet anonymity of "A Lover of Animals" and "Verax."

Discreet anonymity is disagreeable as a rule. The fact was the great Proconsul was in the act of rendering a signal service to the Public; and in consequence the Public did not thank him for his interference. To be sure, it was the first time in his life that he had been guilty of such an indiscretion. This was his first single-handed attempt to render a service to society at large; and, as was only to be expected, society at large was not making itself very pleasant about it.

There could be no doubt that at this moment the great Proconsul was the most unpopular man in London. Old ladies in ermine tippets scowled at him as he passed along Park Lane; and a hostess of mark, famous for her wealth and her humanity, had already crossed him out of her dinner list.

CHAPTER II
TOUCHES UPON A MATTER OF GRAVE PUBLIC IMPORTANCE

OF what crime, do you suppose, has S. of P. been guilty? It was merely that in a public print he had ventured to ask why the payment of the nominal sum of seven and sixpence per annum conferred upon the dogs of London certain privileges in respect of its pavements which society at large, for some little time past, has ceased to claim.

The resources of civilization were ranged already against Shelmerdine of Potterhanworth. Nice-minded women in point lace refused to meet the self-constituted champion of public amenity; the black-velveted mistresses of the Flossies and the Fidos thought the state of his mind must be unpleasant; he was an object of contumely where all that was fair and of good report held sway in the life of the metropolis.

It was a pretty quarrel, and both sides were sustaining it with spirit. The Pro-Darlings, with Verax and a Lover of Animals at their head, had rejoined with mannerly vituperation to the polished sarcasm of the Anti-Darlings. What is your remedy? had inquired the Friends of Fido with a rather obvious sneer. Banish the dumb creation from the pavements of great cities, had replied Inspired Commonsense.

And for our own poor part, Commissioners of the Office of Works, we think that reply is worth a statue.

Verax was making merry though at the expense of a public ornament, and the occupant of Messrs. Maple's best hearthrug, who remembered Verax perfectly well as a grubby infant at his private school, had already formed the pious resolve of putting the fear of God into Verax.

S. of P., having pondered long, sat down at his writing-table; dipped his quill with a certain inherent natural grandeur, and started out on his crushing reply:—"Sir, I have read with amazement the diatribe against my humble and unworthy self which appears under the signature of Verax, to which you have extended the generous hospitality of your columns."

At this point S. of P. bit his quill with such violence that a large blot was shaken from the end of it upon the monogram which decorated the communication.

"The problem as I envisage it"—S. of P. took a small gold pencil out of his waistcoat pocket and made a note on his blotting pad. "The problem as I envisage it"—but the problem that he did envisage was the Suffolk Colthurst, who at that moment entered the room.

The Suffolk Colthurst was large and blonde—so large and so blonde that to a profane mind she rather conveyed the suggestion of a particularly well-grown cauliflower.

"Wally, *please*, don't let me spoil your morning. Don't let me interrupt you, *please*."

The voice of the Suffolk Colthurst was really quite agreeable, although a little light in the upper register. You might even call it flutelike if you cared to indulge in metaphor.

"Not at all, Agatha," said S. of P. with excellent chest resonance. "I am merely envisaging the problem of the—ah—"

"*Don't*, Wally." The voice of the Suffolk Colthurst was perhaps a shade less flutelike if history really calls for these *nuances*. "You are making yourself ridiculous. Please drop the subject."

"No, Agatha." The sun setting over Africa might be compared to the brow of the great Proconsul. "Man in *The Thunderer* most impertinent. Signs himself Verax. Suspect it's that fellow—"

"Wally." The Suffolk Colthurst roared here a little less gently than usual. "I will not uphold you! Everybody thinks it is most injudicious."

"Everybody, Agatha?"

"Paul and Millicent consider—"

"Public health, Agatha, public dec—"

"Wally, once for all, I absolutely refuse to discuss the subject. I will not have you make yourself ridiculous."

The Suffolk Colthurst, with an approximation to natural majesty, put on a pair of gold-rimmed eyeglasses which were suspended round her neck by a cord, and took the Leading Morning Journal off the First Baron's table.

"Impertinent, certainly. Sarcasm, I suppose."

"Suspect it's that fellow Huffham, because I declined to propose him under Rule Two."

"Certainly you do appear to have laid yourself open, but the letter is most ill-natured."

"As though I should be likely to propose him. Known the man all my life."

The Suffolk Colthurst gathered her majestic inches for the ultimatum.

"Wally, you must listen to me. This matter has already gone too far. Let it drop. It is the first time I have known you go out of your way to make yourself ridiculous."

"Public health, Agatha, public decency."

"Leave it to the County Council."

"They are not competent to envisage such a problem as this. And I am determined, in the face of that letter—"

"Paul says that no man can afford to make himself a public laughing-stock."

"Paul's a coward."

"Paul says they are certain to make you an Apostle."

"Eh?"

"If you don't make a fool of yourself."

"Paul said that! Why, pray, should they make me an Apostle?"

"Because there's nobody else; and people will say the race has already passed its zenith if the vacancy is not filled up at once."

"I will say this for Paul—he is well-informed as a rule."

"Wait, Wally, until you are an Apostle."

"Very well then, with the greatest possible reluctance I yield the point for the present. Verax shall wait until—Tell me, Agatha, what have you to say to me?"

The good, the noble—forgive our fervor, O ye Liberal organs of opinion, even if *your* bosoms be not thrilled by this whole-souled devotion to the public weal—the good and noble Shelmerdine of Potterhanworth flung the offending print upon Messrs. Maple's expensive carpet in a sudden uncontrollable access of private pique.

"Agatha." The accents of the great Proconsul were choked with emotion. "Tell me, Agatha, what you have to say to me?"

"Wally," said the Suffolk Colthurst, "what I have to say to you is this."

CHAPTER III
IS DOMESTIC IN THE MAIN, BUT WE HOPE NOT UNWORTHY OF A GREAT CONSTITUTIONAL STATESMAN

WHEN you are up against a serious anticlimax it is a golden rule to begin a fresh chapter.

The Suffolk Colthurst paused, and sat with a further access of natural majesty upon a chair Louis Quinze, supplied, like the hearthrug, by Tottenham Court Road.

"Wally, Philip has declined to come to the Queen's Hall this afternoon to hear Busoni."

Doing his best even in this dangerous anticlimax, S. of P. retrieved the Leading Morning Journal from the carpet, straightened out its crumpled folds with patient humility, laid it on the table, sat down in his own chair—Tottenham Court Road of the best period—put up his eyeglass—by Cary of Pall Mall, maker to the Admiralty—and, in the voice of one pronouncing a benediction, said, "Well, Agatha?"

"Actually declined. Tells me he's engaged to a pantomime at Drury Lane."

"Matter of taste, I suppose."

"Taste, Wally! Dear Adela is coming, and I have taken such trouble to arrange this."

The Proconsul showed a little perturbation.

"No accounting for taste, I presume. Why a man of his age, rising twenty-eight, should prefer—"

"Wally, it is very wrong, and you must speak to him. It is not kind to dear Adela. Please ring the bell."

The Proconsul rang the bell, and a young and very good-looking footman attended the summons.

"Joseph," said his mistress, "if Mr. Philip has not gone yet, tell him, please, that his father would like to see him."

After a lapse of about five minutes, a young man sauntered into the library. He was a somewhat somber-looking young man in a chocolate-colored suiting.

"Good morning, Philip," said the First Baron.

"Mornin', father," said the heir to the barony.

"Philip," said the First Baron, "your mother tells me that you have declined to accompany her and Adela Rocklaw to the Albert Hall this afternoon to hear Paderewski."

The heir to the barony knitted the intellectual forehead that was his by inheritance.

"Not declined, you know, exactly. It's a bit of a mix. I thought the concert was next Saturday." Mr. Philip was a slow and rather heavy young man, but his air was quite sweet and humble, and not without a sort of tacit deference for both parents. "Fact is, I was keepin' next Saturday."

"Why not go this afternoon as you have got wrong in the date? Your mother has been at so much trouble, and I am sure Adela Rocklaw will be disappointed."

"Unfortunately I've fixed up this other thing."

"Engaged to a music hall, I understand."

"Pantomime at Drury Lane," said Philip the sombre.

"Quite so." The Proconsul, like other great men, was slightly impatient of meticulous detail in affairs outside his orbit. "Hardly right, is it, to disappoint Adela Rocklaw, especially after your mother"—Mother, still mounted on the Louis Quinze, sat with eyelids lowered but very level—"has taken so much trouble? At least I, at your age, should not have thought so."

Mr. Philip pondered a little.

"A bit awkward perhaps. I say, Mater, don't you think you could fix up another day?"

The gaze of Mother grew a little less abstract at this invocation.

"Impossible, Phil-ipp"—the Rubens-Minerva countenance, whose ample chin was folded trebly in rolls of adipose tissue was a credit to the Governing Classes—"Dear Adela goes to High Cliff on Wednesday for the shooting."

"Well, I'm sorry," said Mr. Philip quite nicely and politely, "that I shall have to go to Drury Lane this afternoon."

"*Have* to go, Phil-ipp!" Still ampler grew the Governing Classes. "It is really impossible in the circumstances."

"What circumstances, Mater?"

"Dear Adela."

"She won't mind, if you explain. It's like this, you see. Teddy Clapham has taken a box for his kids, and I promised 'em I'd be there—and you can't go back on your word with kids, can you?"

"Why not, Phil-ipp?" inquired the Governing Classes.

"Sort of gives 'em wrong views about things, you know."

"How absurd," said Mother. "Much too sentimental about children nowadays. Telephone to Mr. Clapham and explain the circumstances. I am sure he will understand that as dear Adela is going to High Cliff on Wednesday—"

A cloud gathered on the brow of Philip.

"May be wrong, you know, Mater, but I really can't go back on my word with kids. I promised 'em, you know, and that little Marge is a nailer, and she is only five."

The statement, in spite of its sincerity, did not seem to carry conviction to either parent.

The heir to the barony was a dutiful young man; at least, in an age which has witnessed a somewhat alarming decline in parental authority, he passed as such. His deference, perhaps, was not of a type aggressively old-fashioned, but he honored his father and his mother.

"I'll get a box for the 'Chocolate Soldier' on Monday if you and Adela will come, Mater, but I don't see how I can throw over Teddy Clapham's kids—five of 'em—toddlers—and they ain't got a mother, you know."

"Phil-ipp, this is ridiculous. And dear Adela will be so disappointed, and on Monday there is a reception at the Foreign Office."

"You can go on afterwards."

"But your father and I are engaged to dinner with the Saxmundhams."

"Well, Mater, I'm sorry. I hope you'll explain to Adela. Got mixed in the date and if it hadn't been kids I really would in the circumstances—"

The door knob was now in the hand of the heir to the barony. Parthian bolts were launched at him, but he made good his escape.

"It's a nuisance," he muttered as he closed the door behind him, "but I really don't see what's to be done in the circumstances."

In the entrance hall he put on his hat and was helped by Joseph into an overcoat with an astrachan collar; from the hall stand he took a whanghee cane with massive silver mountings, and sauntered forth pensively to his house of call, that was not very far from the corner of Hamilton Place.

Arrived at that desirable bourn, his first act was to ring up 00494 Wall.

"That you, Teddy? Have you told the kids to feed early to be in time for the risin' of the curtain? Yes, I've bought the Bukit Rajahs. Think so? Yes, not a minute later than a quarter-past one."

Replacing the receiver, the heir to the barony of Shelmerdine of Potterhanworth recruited exhausted nature with a whisky and apollinaris, and put forth from the chaste portals of the Button Club. Adventures were lying in wait for him, however.

As he rounded the corner into Piccadilly, a little unwarily, it must be confessed, he nearly collided with the *Ne Plus Ultra* of fashion in the person of a tall and decidedly smart young woman, in a rather tight black velvet hobble and a charming mutch with a small strip of white fur above the left eyelid.

CHAPTER IV
IN WHICH THE GENTLE READER HAS THE HONOR OF AN INTRODUCTION TO THE SEVENTH UNMARRIED DAUGHTER OF NOT QUITE A HUNDRED EARLS

THE *Ne Plus Ultra* had just achieved the feat of crossing from the Green Park in the charge of a quadruped of whom we are at a loss to furnish a description more explicit. How and why it had been allowed to escape a death by violence at the instance of the passing motor and other mechanically propelled vehicles was yet another of the dark secrets which must be left in the keeping of its Maker.

"Hulloa, Adela!"

Jamming the brakes hard on, the heir to the barony was just able to avert a forcible impact with the fearsome four-footed beast which measured eighteen inches and a quarter from the tip of its tail to the end of its muzzle.

"What is it, Adela? Win it in a raffle?"

The seventh unmarried daughter of not quite a hundred earls was a little inclined to stiffen at this freedom with an Honorable Mention at the Crystal Palace.

"It is a pure-bred rough-haired Himalayan Dust Spaniel, and they are very rare."

"I hope so."

This ill-timed remark did not seem to help the conversation. The seventh unmarried daughter of not quite a hundred earls—she was the daughter of only three earls really, although for that she cannot accept responsibility—tilted her chin to its most aristocratic angle and displayed considerable reserve of manner.

An eyelash, lengthy and sarcastic, flickered upon her cheek.

"Pure-bred rough-coated Himalayan Dust Spaniel," said the heir to the barony. "Stick him in your muff, or you might lose him."

"You are coming to the concert, aren't you?" said the seventh unmarried daughter in a tone singularly detached and cool.

"No, I'm afraid," said the heir to the barony. "Awfully sorry, Adela, but fact is I've got mixed in the day. Thought it was next Saturday."

"Oh, really."

"So I've promised five little kidlets I'd take 'em to the Pantomime at Drury Lane. You don't mind, Adela, do you?—or I say, would you care to come? You'll find it a deal more amusin' than Paderewski. We've got a box, and there'll be any amount of room. And you won't need a chaperone with five kids and their nannas, and the Mater needn't go to Kubelik then, because she hates all decent music worse than I do. Better come, Adela. Pantomime is awfully amusin', and you'll like Clapham if you haven't met him—chap, you know, that married poor little Bridgit Brady."

"Thanks," said the young madam, "but I think I prefer Busoni."

The heir to the barony was rather concerned by the tone of Miss Insolence.

"You aren't rattled, are you, Adela?" said he. "I've made a horrid mess of it, and I'm to blame and all that, but you can't go back on your word with kids, can you? If you come I'm sure you'll like it, and that little Marge is a nailer, and she is only five."

The long-lashed orb from beneath the charming mutch showed very cold and blue.

"Thanks, but I think I prefer Busoni. Come, Fritz."

"Well, I'm sorry," said the penitent heir; and the rather tight hobble and the charming mutch and the pure-bred Himalayan dust spaniel moved round the corner of Hamilton Place in review order.

Humbled and undone, the heir to the barony sauntered up the street, past the Cavalry, past the Savile and past the Bath, until, broken in spirit he stayed his course before the chocolate shop of B. Venoist.

"She's as cross as two sticks," sighed the heir to the barony, as he gazed in at the window. "Always was a muddlin' fool—but you can't go back on your word with kids, can you? Now I must be careful which sort I choose. I expect that sort in pink boxes will make 'em as sick as Monday mornin'."

In this opinion, however, B. Venoist did not concur. He assured the heir to the barony that it was exactly the same quality as that supplied to Buckingham Palace, The Durdans, High Cliff Castle and Eaton Hall.

"If that is so," said the heir to the barony, "I think I'll risk a box." "Looks pretty poisonous," he added—although not to B. Venoist.

"You'll find that all right, sir," said B. Venoist. "Precisely the same quality as supplied to York Cottage."

"I'm glad o' that," said the heir to the barony, disbursing a sum in gold and dangling a large but neat white paper parcel from his index finger.

"Cross as two sticks," mused the stricken young man, putting forth from the chocolate shop of B. Venoist, and bestowing a nod in passing upon a choice light blue striped necktie.

By some odd association of ideas this article of attire was responsible for his course being stayed before his favorite shop window a little farther along the street: to wit, of Mr. Thomas Ling, whose neckties in the opinion of some are as nice as any in London.

"Have you an Old Etonian Association necktie?" he asked of Mr. Thomas Ling, although he knew quite well that Mr. Thomas Ling had, and a Ramblers' also if he had required it.

"The narrow or the broad, sir?" said Mr. Thomas Ling.

"The broad," said the heir to the barony; but at Mr. Thomas Ling's look of frank incredulity, he corrected it to "the narrow."

Armed with the narrow, the heir to the barony left the shop of Mr. Thomas Ling poorer by the sum of five and sixpence, and also by a box of the best assorted chocolates from B. Venoist which he had the misfortune to leave upon the counter.

"Cross as two sticks," muttered the stricken young man as he reached the very end of the celebrated thoroughfare, and gazed an instant into the window of Messrs. Wan & Sedgar to see how their famous annual winter sale was getting on in the absence of the winter.

The mind of the heir to the barony hovered not unpleasantly, for all its unhappiness, over a peculiarly chaste display of silk and woolen pajamas, three pairs for two guineas, guaranteed unshrinkable, when with a shock he awoke to the fact that he was no longer the proud possessor of a box of the best assorted chocolates from B. Venoist.

"I'm all to pieces this mornin'," registered the vain young man on the inner tablets of his nature. Thereupon he took out his watch, a gold hunting repeater, a present from his mother when he came of age, and in a succinct form apostrophized his Maker.

"My God! nine minutes to one and I've got to collect the kids from Eaton Place and the bally show begins at one-thirty. Here, I say!"

The heir to the barony hailed a passing taxi.

"Call at Ling's up on the right, and then drive like the devil to 300 Eaton Place."

"Right you are, sir," said the driver of the taxi, in such flagrant contravention of the spirit of the Public Vehicles Act 9 Edwardus VII Cap III that we much regret being unable to remember his number.

It was the work of two minutes for the heir to the barony to retrieve the box of best assorted chocolates from the custody of Mr. Thomas Ling up on the right, and then the driver of the taxi sat down in the saddle and was just proceeding to let her out a bit, in accordance with instructions, when Constable X held him up peremptorily at the point where Bond Street converges upon B. Venoist. Not, however, we are sorry to say, in order to take the number of this wicked chauffeur, engaged in breaking an Act of Parliament for purposes of private emolument, but merely to enable an old lady in a stole of black mink and a black hat with white trimmings, together with a Pekinese sleeve dog, lately the property of the Empress of China, to cross the street and buy a box of water colors for her youngest nephew.

Certainly she was a very dear old lady; but the heir to the barony cursed her bitterly, as, gold hunting repeater in hand, he vowed that the kids would not be in time for the rising of the curtain. Part of his blame overflowed upon the head of Constable X; and we ourselves concur in this, because we certainly think that, if stop the traffic he must, it behooved him, as the appointed guardian of the public peace, to take the number of this guilty chauffeur.

As it was, the driver of the taxi, owing to this dereliction of duty upon the part of Constable X—a kind man certainly, and about to become a sergeant—sat down again in the saddle and proceeded to let her out a bit further. So that anon, swinging along that perilous place where four-and-twenty metropolitan ways converge, yclept Hyde Park Corner, he came within an ace of running down a perfectly blameless young man in an old bowler hat and a reach-me-down, the author of this narrative, who was on his way to consult with his respected publisher as to whether a work of ripe philosophy would do as well in the autumn as in the spring.

The young man in the old bowler hat—old but good of its kind, purchased of Mr. Lock in the street of Saint James on the strength of "the success of the spring season" (for the reach-me-down no defense is offered)—the young man in the old bowler hat stepped back on to the pavement with as much agility as an old footballer's knee would permit, and cursed the occupant of the taxi by all his gods for a bloated plutocrat, and in the unworthy spirit of revenge vowed to make him the hero of his very next novel.

A cruel revenge, but not, we think, unjustified. Idle rich young fellow—toiled not, neither did he spin—nursing a gold hunting repeater in a coat with an astrachan collar and one of Messrs. Scott's latest—with a red face and a suspicion of fur upon the upper lip—taking five kids who had lost their mother to the pantomime without his lunch—how dare he run down a true pillar of democracy at the rate of thirty-five miles an hour!

At nine minutes past one by the gold hunting repeater, in the middle of Victoria Street, the hard thought occurred to the young man that he would get no lunch. Still, let us not overdo our regard for his heroism. He had not finished his breakfast until something after eleven, and his breakfast had consisted of three devilled kidneys on toast, a plate of porridge, a grilled sole, muffins, marmalade and fruit *ad libitum*, but still the young chap was undoubtedly going to miss his luncheon.

At twelve minutes past one by the gold hunting repeater, the heir to the barony was acclaimed in triumph from the threshold of Number 300 Eaton Place by five kids and their nannas, who were beginning almost to fear that Uncle Phil had forgotten to call for 'em.

"It is only Aunty Cathy that forgets," said Marge, who, considering that at present she is only five, has excellent powers of observation. "Uncle Phil never forgets nothink."

Shrill cheers greeted the idle, rich young fellow. Blow, blow thy whistle, Butler. Let us have another taxi up at once. Marge and Timothy and Alice Clara in taxi the first with Uncle Phil; Nannas Helen and Lucy with Dick and the Babe in taxi the second.

"Must be at Drury Lane," said Uncle Phil to Messieurs les Chauffeurs, "before the risin' of the curtain at one-thirty."

Those grim evil-doers nodded darkly, and away they tootle-tootled round the corner into the Buckingham Palace Road. One fourteen, said the gold hunting repeater. Bar accidents, we shall do it on our heads.

"Oh, Uncle Phil," said Marge, "we've forgotten Daddy."

"Comin' on from the city," said Uncle Phil.

CHAPTER V
IN WHICH THE GENTLE READER IS TAKEN TO THE PANTOMIME IN THE COMPANY OF MARGE AND TIMOTHY AND ALICE CLARA AND DICK AND THE BABE AND HELEN AND LUCY NANNA, AND WE HOPE YOU'LL ENJOY IT AS MUCH AS THEY DID

THE door of Marge's taxi was opened by a benevolent bewhiskered policeman, who, being himself a family man, lifted her out as if he was pleased to see her. Uncle Phil then handed out Timothy and Alice Clara; and then he got out himself and performed an action which we are forced to view with regret. He opened the little purse which he kept in the pocket opposite to the gold hunting repeater, and presented a whole "bar" to the member of the criminal classes whose number we have so unfortunately omitted to take. And that dark-visaged misdemeanant, who, if every man had had his due would have had the blood of half the West End of London on what he was pleased to call his conscience, spat for luck on his guilty emolument when no one was looking, and thought of the new hat he would be able to buy the missus. At least we hope he did, although Mr. G-lsw-rthy rather has his doubts.

Shoals of other kids were converging upon the portals of Drury; kids in taxis, kids in growlers, kids on foot. It was 1:28, and all were frightfully anxious to be in their places by the time the curtain—the real, not the fireproof curtain—went up. Timothy and Alice Clara were inclined to hustle round a bit, but Marge had such implicit faith in Uncle Phil that to her mind hustling was not called for and was therefore unladylike.

In justice to Marge, it is only fair to say that her faith in Uncle Phil was justified. Crowds of arrivals were in the vestibules; kids with their fathers, kids with their mothers, kids with their nannas, kids with their maiden aunts. But straight as a die Uncle Phil cut out a course for his convoy. In double file his party of seven—five kids and two quite nice-looking nannas—followed in the wake of his astrachan collar and whanghee cane with silver mountings. At 1:29 Marge was seated in Box B, next to the stage and on a level with the dress circle. Timothy and Alice Clara and Dick and the Babe were seated beside her—certainly a great triumph for all concerned, including the criminal eating his dinner out of his handkerchief within a stone's throw of the editorial office of the *Spectator*.

Uncle Phil bought a programme and paid a shilling for it, although sixpence was the price.

"Cinderella, I see. Rippin'."

Marge knew it was Cinderella. She had dreamed that it was. Besides all the best pantomimes are Cinderella. But where was Daddy? Why didn't he make haste? There was Mr. Lover—loud applause—the orchestra was tuning up. Oh, why didn't Daddy—

Oh, joy! Oh, providence! Daddy came into Box B just as Marge was inquiring for him, in his tall hat, fresh from Mincing Lane. A rather tired and sad-looking Daddy, a little hollow in the cheeks and with rings under his eyes, although fortunately Marge didn't notice them. But as soon as he caught sight of the heir to the barony, which his other name is Uncle Phil, a smile seemed to come right over him.

"Damned good of you, old boy," he said, as he hung up his tall hat beside the very latest performance on the part of Messrs. Scott. "Ungodly hour to begin," said Daddy. "Hope you got your lunch all right."

"Ra-*ther*," said Uncle Phil. "You?"

"Oh, ye-es."

We know what Uncle Phil is, and we are afraid we must say the same of Father.

But Mr. Lover is already under way with his overture.

And then Father asked Marge if she could see, and if Timothy could see, and was the Babe comfortable, and other well-meaning but superfluous questions, almost as it were to convey a sense of his importance. And there was the curtain actually going up, on a field of new-mown hay. It was magnificent, but, with all respect to Mr. Hollins, the scent of the hay was only just able to get across the footlights. But don't let Mr. Hollins take it to heart, because Marge, quite one of the most important people in all his noble theater, was able to smell the scent of the new-mown hay all right.

"A toppin' good chorus," said Uncle Phil.

Put that plume in your cap, Mr. Hollins, because no young man of his years in London has had more theatrical experience than the heir to the barony. So lately as the Monday previous he had made his forty-sixth appearance at *Our Miss Gibbs*. Hunting chorus, too, though what the followers of the chase were doing in a field of new-mown hay—but after all, what's the use of being in Arcady if you can't have things exactly as you want 'em?

Dick and the Babe fairly crowed with pleasure. Helen Nanna hoped they would restrain themselves, and whispered to Lucy Nanna that *never* had she seen anything like it. And while she was whispering this truth to Lucy Nanna there came a roar from the house, and an oldish, middle-aged person sauntered into the field of new-mown hay, immediately tripped over herself, and assured all whom it might concern that she was a perfect lady. She then proceeded to sing a song about a gentleman of the name of Kelly.

The enthusiasm that was caused by her song and behavior would be vain to describe.

"Chap's a genius," said Father. "Who is he?"

"Wilkie Bard, of course," said Uncle Phil.

"Has anybody here seen Kelly?" inquired the old lady. It appeared that every single person there, including the occupants of Box B, either had seen or hoped to see Kelly.

And then quite suddenly the lights went out, the orchestra rolled in semi-darkness, something happened to the scenery, the lights went up again, and there was a kitchen in the ancestral halls of Baron de No-Cash.

Again crowed the Babe with pleasure, and he had a perfect right to do so; because it was really a remarkable sort of a kitchen, larger by far than the one in Eaton Place where cook kept the marmalade; though, doubtless, what most intrigued the fancy of the Babe was the enormous fireplace which had accommodation for a turnspit and at least twenty-four persons.

In the temporary absence of any single human individual the turnspit had the stage all to itself. This was a subtle device on the part of the management. An air of rapt expectation enfolded the great audience, as of something going to happen.

And something did.

A perfect roar of enthusiasm heralded the happening of the something. Now what do you suppose it was? Nothing less than the arrival of the Principal Girl.

She just wandered in, no-how as it were, with a broom in her hand and her skirt in tatters, and a red cap over her curls and her feet in slippers. She was merely the maid of all work in the kitchen of the Baron de No-Cash, a downtrodden creature according to legend and according to the libretto, but you would hardly have thought so, since she had to stand bowing for two whole minutes over her broom handle before she was allowed to proceed with the business of life.

The roar reverberated from the roof of the gallery to the floor of the pit. Kids in boxes, kids in stalls, kids in the dress circle, and an infant in arms at the back of the pit all did their best; and responsible middle-aged gentlemen from the Kaffir Circus and the Rubber Market, a grandee from the Home Department, a judge of the Court of King's Bench, a solicitor who had applied the money of his clients to his own purposes, although nobody had found him out at present, a substantial family from Hammersmith, the proprietor of a flourishing Brixton laundry, whose eldest girl was in the ballet, an old charwoman in the front row of the gods, and a thousand and one other heterogeneous elements whom we are only able to refer to in the most general terms, assisted Marge and Timothy and Alice Clara, and Dick and the Babe to make the welkin behave frightfully foolish, over a rather plain-looking girl of twenty-four who had to keep bowing over her broom handle before she could get on with the business of life.

And when at last she was able to get on with the business of life, what do you suppose it was? Why, to sing, of course, "Come with me to Arcadee." What in the world else do you suppose her business in life could be?

A little well-timed assistance from Mr. Lover, which she really didn't require, and away she soared straight up through the middle register, and at the same moment something seemed to go ping, ping, beneath the knitted waistcoat of chocolate worsted of the heir to the barony, standing at the back of Box B by the side of Father.

"Come with me to Arcadee."

Uncle Phil accepted her invitation without the slightest hesitation—we are not so sure as we should like to be about Father—but Nannas Helen and Lucy, and Marge and the rest of 'em, indeed an overwhelming majority of that crowded and representative assembly, went straight to Arcadee with that rather plain young woman who was suffering from a cold in the head.

We call her plain as much out of deference to Mr. G-lsw-rthy, and Mr. H. G. W-lls and Mr. Arnold B-nn-tt as any other reason we can think of. Because in the opinion of the heir to the barony she was already enshrined as "a nailer," and no girl absolutely and unmistakably plain could possibly have been granted the highest of all diplomas by one of such a ripe experience of all phases and degrees of womanhood.

No, Mr. G-lsw-rthy, perhaps not a patrician beauty, like the daughter of whom we wot, still *plain* is not the word exactly. Can you call any young woman plain, who, attired in her nondescript manner, hypnotizes the whole of Drury with her tiny handkerchief edged with lace, every time she plucks it out of her tatterdemalia?

Plain?—no, sir, decidedly not. A plain girl could never hypnotize the whole of Drury with her handkerchief, including an austere old gentleman in the second row of the stalls, allowing a question of taxed costs to stand over till the following Tuesday. Plain, Mr. G-lsw-rthy!—we at least, and the heir to the barony are forced to dissent.

"She's a nailer. What's her name?" said Uncle Phil.

Father lowered his sombre eyes, and shook his head at Uncle Philip. He had not gone to Arcadee with the Principal Girl, you see. Upon a day another Principal Girl had lured him thither, and Father had had to come back again, and Father was feeling that he wanted never to go any more to Arcadee—except with the Principal, Principal Girl.

Helen Nanna, a good, kind girl and high up in the class at Old Dame Nature's Select Academy for Young Ladies, handed the programme to Uncle Philip, who perused the same as soon as the vibrations under the chocolate waistcoat would allow him to do so.

"Birdie Brightwing—no, she's Prince Charming, and this is Cinderella. Mary Caspar is Cinderella."

Uncle Philip, for all his ripe experience, had never heard of Miss Caspar, and Father hadn't either. Never been seen at the Gaiety or the Lyric. No wonder a star had had to be placed by the Management opposite the name of Miss Caspar to denote an explanatory footnote at the bottom of the programme.

"By special arrangement with the Royal Italian Opera House, Blackhampton."

Ha! that explained it. Deep minds were in this. Merely one more stroke of genius on the part of Mr. Hollins. When Florence de Vere had broken her engagement at the eleventh hour in order to take part in the Beauchamp Season, to the dismay of all that was best in the life of the metropolis, what did Mr. Hollins do? Sit down and twiddle his thumbs, did he? Not so, my masters. He called for his coat with the beaver collar, and his new bowler hat from Mr. Lock, and he took a first-class ticket for the Royal Italian Opera House, Blackhampton.

"Not for the King of England, not me," said the Lessee and Manager haughtily. "We open on Boxin' Night with *Aladdin*, and the bills are printed."

Oh, vain Lessee! Little he recked of the Napoleonic faculty of Mr. Hollins in combination with his cheque-book. Meetings of indignation were held in Blackhampton and its environs, but after all, the loss of the famous midland city was the gain of the great metropolis.

Miss Caspar had come, had been seen, had overcome.

"'Core!" roared the bloods in the stalls.

"'Core!" echoed the cads in the pit.

"'Core!" cried the young ladies in the dress circle.

"'Core!" yelled the members of nature's nobility, cheek by jowl with the magnificent ceiling.

Mary Caspar's cold was really frightful, but she couldn't help herself, poor girl. Once more she took 'em all to Arcadee—Marge and Timothy and Alice Clara and Dick and the Babe and Helen and Lucy Nanna and certainly Uncle Phil. As for poor Father, he leaned back against the wall with his hands in his pockets, and almost wished he hadn't come. There was something about that girl taking 'em all to Arcadee that somehow—no, dash it all, he must learn to keep that upper lip a bit stiffer.

"'Core!" shouted Father—but so feebly that nobody heard him.

"Only a hundred a week," said Mr. Hollins in the ear of the Chairman of the Syndicate in the box below. "Dirt cheap."

"Sign her for five years at double the salary," said the Chairman of the Syndicate in the ear of the famous manager.

"Nothing like a provincial training," said Mr. Hollins. "Teaches 'em how to get right home to the heart of the people."

"'Core!" roared the Chairman of the Syndicate.

"Absolute nailer," said Uncle Phil.

And then her acting! It was so perfectly easy and natural that it really didn't seem like acting at all. Her speaking voice, for all that it hurt her so, was clear and low and quite agreeable; and wiser men than Uncle Phil have thought that such a voice as that is the greatest charm in any young woman. Not quite so ultra-refined perhaps as that of the seventh unmarried daughter of not quite a hundred earls; not quite so much torture was inflicted upon the letter "o," that honest vocable. Icy tones had been Adela's that morning in the opinion of the heir to the barony; those of the new-risen star of Blackhampton were clear and unaffected and ringing with human sympathy. No wonder that the sensitive mechanism behind the chocolate waistcoat was thrown clean out of gear.

She acted beautifully that fine scene inside the fireplace with a nondescript entity, by the name of Buttons, which his proper name is Mr. Graves and a man of genius; acted it beautifully during the time her wicked sisters had left her at home to work like a menial while they had gone to the Prince Charming's ball.

After the Principal Girl had sung another ballad, to the entire satisfaction of all that was best in the life of the metropolis, the great and good Mr. Lover handed up to her a noble box of chocolates from an unknown friend in front.

The appearance of this rare box of chocolates struck the heir to the barony with deep dismay. What had happened to the ill-fated box he had bought of B. Venoist!

"I'm hanged," he said, "if I haven't left that bally box in the taxi after all!"

The heir to the barony waited until the Principal Girl had retired to get into her famous glass slippers and her ballroom kit, and then like a thief in the night he stole out of Box B, that none should see him go, and crept round the back of the dress circle to the refreshment buffet presided over by a Hebe of three-and-forty summers in an outfit of yellow curls.

He would never be able to forgive himself if the kids should think he had forgotten those chocolates.

"Price o' those?"

The heir to the barony disbursed the sum with his accustomed munificence.

"Hullo, young feller, what are you doing *here*?"

This question was asked by a gentleman of prosperous appearance who was holding up a yellow fluid in a tiny glass and looking as though he might presently imbibe it.

"Party o' kids," said the heir to the barony. "Toppin' good show."

The gentleman of the prosperous appearance quite agreed and invited him civilly to drink.

"Must get back with this," said the heir to the barony, holding up a very fine performance on the part of good Messrs. Cadbury.

Although the heir to the barony stayed not to partake of liquid refreshment at the expense of the gentleman at the buffet, and rightly so, we think, having regard to the tragedy of B. Venoist, yet the latter, who was engaged in recruiting exhausted nature with a sherry and angostura bitters, was one of the most distinguished men throughout the length and breadth of the metropolis. Arminius Wingrove was the name of him; a man of consequence to this narrative as to many another one; envied by some, yet esteemed by all who knew him, inasmuch as he was one of the leading dramatic authors of the period. More of him anon. But please to remember, when the time arrives, that you have already had the honor of a formal introduction to Arminius Wingrove.

The slave of duty stole back to Box B, and his reappearance with the signal triumph of Messrs. Cadbury went entirely unmarked, his luck being such that he crept in at the moment the Fairy Godmother waved her wand, and the rats and mice, not to mention the lizards, became piebald ponies who bore off Cinderella in her state chariot to the Prince's Ball.

Helen and Lucy Nanna had never seen anything like it—never; the Babe crowed with pleasure; Marge and Timothy and Alice Clara could merely gasp; and Father confided to Uncle Phil in a sombre undertone that it was the best pantomime he had seen for years.

We give Mr. Hollins our grateful and cordial meed for Part I of his noble annual production, what time the fire-proof curtain falls upon salvos of wild applause, in order that the ladies of the ballet may change their clothing, and the orchestra may remove the froth from a pint of bitter, and Mary Caspar, brave girl and true-blue she-Briton, every inch of her, may drink a much-needed cup of tea; while Marge and Timothy and Alice Clara and Dick and the Babe and the rest of 'em obtain first hand information as to what that box is that Uncle Phil has acquired by barter from good Messieurs Cadburyee for the sum of three half-crowns.

Dick fancies the pink one. Can't have it, because it ain't cricket for kids of three to take precedence of grown-up ladies rising five. Pipe his eyes, does he? Not so, my masters—the yellow one is just as agreeable to Master Richard who will probably play for Middlesex in after life. Timothy thinks that the one with the walnuts on it—if Marge don't mind. Marge don't mind, because there is another one with walnuts on it; but even if it stood alone she'd say she didn't, not that there is any particular credit due to her, it simply being that she's kind of made like that.

Helen Nanna preferred the plain. She had never tasted anything nicer. Lucy Nanna fancied the one with the nougat in it. Daddy didn't care for choc-o-lates. As for Uncle Phil, the munificent donor who had missed his luncheon, although no one knew it besides himself, he took a peppermint warily, but found it quite all right.

But there is the orchestra blaring like a giant refreshed with wine; and in respect of the great Mr. Lover this is no more than sober verity, since, at the instance of a friend and admirer, he had been to interview Hebe with yellow curls. Boomed and blared the cornets to hail the reappearance of the ladies of the ballet, in canary-colored stockings which had no clocks upon 'em. Austere old gentleman, second row of stalls, letting question of taxed costs, etc., dived for opera glasses, for which he had duly disbursed the fee of sixpence as by law prescribed.

Ping went the clockwork under the chocolate waistcoat of Uncle Philip. There she was again. What a dream she was in her golden chariot with a diadem over her chestnut curls. Bowed and kissed her hand to the admiring multitude; stepped down from her chariot, smiling, smiling in her royal manner at the footmen as she passed them, and followed by all that was best in the life of the metropolis as she crossed the threshold of the Prince's domicile.

Ping went the heart of Uncle Philip. Austere old gentleman fumbled for his programme—dear old boy lamenting his wretched memory for names. Bald-headed light of the Chancery Bar unfolds his pince-nez; outspoken youth in gallery roars out "*Good* on yer, Mary!"

In our humble judgment outspoken youth was quite correct. O ye Maries of England, you ought to be proud of her! Trumpets blared, lights went out, transformation to Fairyland, and there again was Mary! Once again she was going to let the painter go.

O ye Maries of England, true heroism is not the private perquisite of the Royal Horse Guards Blue. The precious seed is in you all, my dears. May you always do your respective duties as this particular Mary did when England expects it of you.

Right up she went through the middle register, tearing her poor throat to pieces at every note she took. Fairly launched the painter—"Nelson and his Gentlemen in Blue." Don't know whose the words are—Swinburne maybe, or Campbell Thomas, or Dibdin, or Gilbert W. S.; music may have been by Brahms or Schubert, or Strauss or Wagner or Debussy, but critics of Leading Morning Journal seem to think by none of these.

"'Core!" roared the cads in the stalls.

"'Core!" yelled the bloods in the pit.

"'Core!" cried the young ladies in the dress circle.

"'Core!" roared the members of nature's nobility all over the house.

"Right on the spot all the time," said the Chairman of the Syndicate. "Hollins, have that five years' contract put in hand at once."

"Aye, aye, sir," said Hollins, forgetting the degree to which it had pleased providence to call him in the lilt of that nautical tune.

"*Good* on yer, Mary," proclaimed outspoken youth with almost pathetic enthusiasm from the front row of the gods.

At the end of the twenty-fourth verse Mr. Lover presented a bouquet of lilies of the valley, smilax and maidenhair fern to this national heroine. Paid for by the management, saith young friend of the *Standard News*. May be, young sir, but Marge waved frantically; and the Babe crowed shrilly, and Uncle Philip deplored the fact that he had not had the sense to bring one himself.

We pray of your patience, gentles all, to retain your seats until the Principal Girl has married the Prince. She won't be long now, that good, brave girl. How she has done it we don't quite know; and remember, people, what British pluck has already done this afternoon, British pluck will have to do all over again this evening.

"Girl ought to be in bed," says Harley Street Physician in box, opposite Box B, to old college friend the house surgeon at Bart's. "She'll have a temperature if she isn't careful."

"She's given the house a temperature all right," said the house surgeon at Bart's, mingling refined humor with grave thoughts like the American judge at the funeral of his mother-in-law.

Kids staying of course for the end of it all. Details much too banal to inflict upon the overwrought patience of the gentle reader. But Father and Uncle Phil, lunchless and thirsty, patient and uncomplaining, though bored to tears, stand as ever at the back of Box B, at the post of duty. Whole-hoggers these upright citizens, though one was the eldest son of a peer and the other connected by marriage with several. But let justice be done to 'em. They would see it all out to the end, in order that Marge and Timothy and Alice Clara and the Babe and Helen and Lucy Nanna should be sent back in taxis to Number 300 Eaton Place, just as they ought to be.

Father's handicap was four at Prince's, and he would have much preferred to spend his only free afternoon that week at Mitcham where the common is, and where you can lose a golf ball about as soon as in any other rural spot in Surrey. As for the heir to the barony, as all the world doth know, his path as designed for him that afternoon by the lady his mother, was the Queen's Hall by Portland Place—that temple of elevated and serious energy, wherein Busoni had designed to charm—and we hope he would be able to do so—the seventh unmarried daughter of not quite a hundred earls.

Don't think us forward, O ye Liberal organs of opinion, for mentioning details so trite as these; but observe that young plutocrat, that idle, rich young fellow, with astrachan collar and whanghee cane, white spats by Grant and Cockburn, bowler hat by Messrs. Scott—observe him conducting that convoy of motherless kids and their nannas, as simply and politely as though he was the father of 'em—and may he one day have five kids and two quite nice-looking nannas of his own!—conducting 'em through kids in cloaks, kids in mufflers, kids in hats and kids without 'em; through the seething vestibule of Drury, down the steps and round the corner; watch him hail an honest but ill-favored, likewise a dishonest but better favored, motor man. Watch him pack 'em in and give directions, assisted by the unsought attentions of a Distinguished Member of the Great Unwashed.

"Three hundred Eaton Place. Drive slowly."

Oh, Irony!

Seeks to find a small piece of silver for the Great Unwashed. Can discover four pence merely. Tempered gratitude on part of Great Unwashed. A real Toff never condescends beneath a tanner; and if he hasn't got one, why, what's the matter with a bob?

"Time for a game of pills before dinner?" says the heir to the barony.

"'Fraid there won't be time, old boy," says Father. "Letters to attend to."

"Time for a drink at the Betterton, anyhow," says Uncle Philip.

That temple of aristocratic Bohemia, at which monarchs sup and which actor managers frequent, is in such close proximity to Drury, that only plutocracy in its most aggravated form would have called for a taxi in order to get to it. But what can you expect, O ye Liberal organs of opinion, from the heir to a Tory peerage!

CHAPTER VI
IN WHICH WE DINE OUT IN GROSVENOR SQUARE

FATHER sat down to write a letter, and Uncle Philip smoked a cigarette in a meerschaum holder and read the *Sporting Times*. But the unfortunate young man could hardly bring his mind to bear upon those chaste pink pages for all that the Dwarf and Mr. Pitcher were quite at the top of their form this week.

Was it that his conscience hurt him? Fretting about Busoni do you suppose? Wondering whether the seventh unmarried daughter and the dearest mother had got to Queen's Hall unscathed, and had also managed to get back again all right?

May have been so. If there is a doubt about it, conscientious fellow is entitled to benefit thereby; but we are bound to admit there is a doubt upon the subject.

And our reasons be these, lieges all and masterful men. At twenty to seven, long before Father had finished his letters, who should deign to enter the silence room but the identical Arminius Wingrove, to whom the gentle reader has already had the honor of a formal introduction.

Ping went the heart of the heir to the barony. He rose from his chair of russia leather, lately recovered at the behest of the Committee, and trod softly across the turkey carpet, old but good.

"Fathead," said the heir to the barony—for this coarse familiarity we can only offer the excuse that the Great Man had always been Fathead to his familiars since his Oxford days—"Fathead," said the heir to the barony, "I want to talk to you."

Fathead almost looked as though he had no desire to converse with the too-familiar groundling, being due to take the Dowager Duchess of Bayswater to dine at the Ritz Hotel.

But on all occasions Arminius knew how to assume the air of the *bon camarade*.

"Fire away. Only five minutes. Dining old Polly Bayswater at the Ritz."

"More fool you," said the profane young man.

Alas! that nothing is sacred to the helots of the Button Club.

"Come into the smoking-room, where we can talk a bit."

"Five minutes only," said Arminius Wingrove, fixing his eyeglass with his accustomed air of mental power.

The heir to the barony laid hold of the arm of the famous dramatist, as though he didn't intend to let it go; hustled him into a room adjoining, deposited him in the emptiest corner, ordered two sherries and angostura bitters, and straightway proceeded to show what comes of spending Saturday afternoon in places licensed by the Lord Chamberlain for stage performances.

"Do you know by any chance the girl who was Cinderella?"

Superfluous question to ask of Arminius Wingrove, we can tell you that. Are you not aware that the young person who played Cinderella had already captured all that was best in the life of the metropolis? What a question to ask Arminius Wingrove who knew every man, woman, and infant phenomenon worthy of regard, from Anna Maria, Duchess Dowager of Bayswater, to the ticket inspector on the Vauxhall trams.

"Know her? Of course I know her. And it was I who chose her first long-clothes for her." At least the air of bland surprise of Arminius Wingrove was open to that interpretation, although, of course, modesty would have restrained him from saying anything of the kind. "Everybody knows her—*now*."

"Didn't know she was famous," said the heir to the barony, limp as rags.

Arminius measured him in his naïveté, though not with the naked eye.

"Absolute nailer," said the heir to the barony.

All *vieux jeu* to Arminius W. Took out his watch—inset with jewels of rare variety—a present from—never mind who, ye froward journalists.

"Ritz at eight. Polly will curse if kept waiting for her meals."

"Absolute nailer," said the vain young man. "Would like to meet her awfully if you can manage it for me."

Arminius Wingrove pondered some.

"Why—ye-es," said that great man.

"Thought perhaps?"

Arminius Wingrove pondered more.

"Must go—poor old Polly. But be at the Carlton Monday at five."

With suppressed, but deep and sincere, emotion the heir to the barony wrung the bejeweled hand of Arminius Wingrove. Never more would he pull his leg. Not a bad chap; harmless very.

"Have another sherry?"

Nary.

Exit Arminius Wingrove to dress to take old Polly to the Ritz Hotel. Let us hope his evenin' will not be as dull as in his heart of hearts he fears it will be; and even if he is carried out a corpse at a quarter-past eleven from that palatial building which is not so far from Piccadilly, his dying thought must be that he perished in the performance of a kind, considerate, and gentlemanly action.

Not of course, my lords and gentlemen, that it was the first he had performed by many.

The plutocrat was dining, too. With whom? inquires Transatlantic Journalist. With his people, of course, in Grosvenor Square. Not at all romantic. Wasn't it, though? Adela and her Pa were going, although Pa never went anywhere since the rheumatism.

Nobody else; just *en famille*. Something in the air? *Does* look rather like it, doesn't it, Cousin? A little previous perhaps; and it doesn't do to be too previous, even in modern journalism.

Dressed in the Albany in his tightest evening trousers did this idle, rich young fellow; although the question why he could not have performed that action under the roof of his excellent parents at No. 88 Grosvenor Square, the corner house, can only be answered on the plain hypothesis that his uncle and aunts and other collaterals had left him a great deal of money to play with.

White waistcoat, of course; buttons mother o' pearl; tie by Mr. Thomas Ling; pomade by Truefitt for the upper story. Even his man was proud of him. But we grieve to relate that his reception at No. 88 Grosvenor Square, the corner house, was not so cordial as it might have been, considering that up to the time of writing the life of this idle, rich young fellow was void of serious blemishes.

He could feel the frost even before he took off the coat with the astrachan collar.

"Ought to keep a stove, Jenkins, in this hall during the winter months."

But that well-trained servitor looked solemnly down his Wellington nose, because even he could perceive that the temperature that was already up against Master Philip had nothing whatever to do with the state of the British climate.

"Lady Adela and his lordship 'ave been here a quarter of a hower, sir."

What! twenty past eight. O curst pantomime of Drury! O curst vision in thy chestnut curls, that thou shouldst annihilate time and space for a comparatively recent creation—although a Tory one, happily!

"I look like getting it in the neck properly," said the vain young fellow for his personal private information; and Mr. Jenkins, that well-trained servitor, who heard him not, would yet have concurred had he happened to do so.

Certainly this surmise was fairly accurate. Adela's gaze was very cool and level; her method of voice production also enhanced her statuesque appearance. Even her Pa looked the reverse of cordial, but that of course, was rheumatism.

Such a pity he had missed Busoni, said the good old Mater. *Dear* Adela had enjoyed the Second Rhapsodie of Liszt *so* much.

Pa's seventh daughter may have done so, but her demeanor seemed rather to make a secret of the information.

Certainly have to take to Jaeger underclothing, now that the frost had come at last. Shivered poor young fellow, as he took in Adela in sequins, a frock he had seen her in before.

Cross as two sticks. Oh, yes, a proper minx. If she will go on like this, we shall really have to see about a boor who will abuse her.

Pa talked high politics with First Baron: whether it was merely fun of Wilhelm, or whether Wilhelm *weally* meant it.

"We will keep our eyes upon him," said these two distinguished compeers of Mr. Harold Box.

"Dear Adela," said the good old Mater, "don't you think that Elektra is quite the finest music that Wagner has ever written?"

Dear Adela didn't really know. In fact she didn't seem to care about Elektra, or about Busoni, or about Sir Henry Wood. Seemed to think that salted almonds and Burgundy were of more importance far, although we are bound to say that we think dear Adela was wrong in this.

Of course it was up to Mr. Philip, as a man of birth and education to have a word or two to say. But unluckily for him, in the stress of his laudable ambition, he suddenly slipped his bridle, and waltzed right into the conversation.

It was not so much lack of tact as the act of destiny. He could be as tactful as another previous to attending this ill-fated matinée at Drury Lane; but since that tragic action he was merely one more tempest-tossed mortal—for all the *soigné* look he had—in the grim toils of fate.

"I wish you *had* come, Adela, really," said the vain young man. "There was a girl there playing Cinderella!"

"*How* interesting," said the good old Mater.

Adela nibbled a salted almond pensively.

"Absolute nailer," said Mr. Philip.

"How *very* interesting. And Busoni's first piece was the overture to the polonaise by Chopin—quite classical, of course, but so full of verve and charm."

"Her name is Mary Caspar, and Teddy Clapham hadn't heard of her before."

"What a strain it must be for those poor professionals. It made one quite ill to watch Busoni. Poor man got so excited, but a *polonaise* in such a *difficult* form of music, one understands."

"'Nelson and his Boys in Blue' was absolutely rippin'. I say, Mater, if you have some free afternoon, Saturday or Wednesday, I should like you and Adela to come and hear her sing it, awfully."

"And Sir Henry Wood conducted so admirably, didn't he, Adela dear?"

"I suppose he is a good conductor," said Adela. "But music is so tiresome unless one happens to be musical, and even then one is likely to be bored."

"Ought to have come to Cinderella," said Mr. Philip. "Enjoyed it awfully, I'm sure. An absolute nailer. I mean to go again."

Even with a weight-for-age allowance for the tact, the charm, and the urbanity of one of London's leading Constitutional hostesses, it would be idle to speak of the evening as a great success. The good old Mater did all that a brave woman and a devoted mother could have done in the circumstances, but such was the atmospheric pressure that at last she was obliged to ask the butler whether anything had gone wrong with the ventilator of the new fire grate, which she had always viewed with suspicion from the moment it had been put in.

In the withdrawing-room the frost grew worse.

"I must really have my cloak," said the mother of the heir.

Vain to stir the fire; nought could uncongeal the atmosphere. No, it was not one of your successes, Mater; no use pretending, is it? Better face the facts, but you are not to blame, my dear. From the first you have acted in simple good faith, in accord with your excellent Suffolk Colthurst instincts; and they are very safe things to go by as a rule.

It was right and kind of you to help dear Adela to take up the problem of a young man who had rather more money than was good for him, and who would be all the better for having a nice sensible girl to spend it for him. And we are free to admit that Adela was capable of making herself uncommonly useful in that way if only she would have brought her mind to bear upon the subject.

Please don't jump to such hasty conclusions, says a Feminine Reader at this point—alas! that we have so few. When sir, you suggest that dear Adela was not allowing her mind to bear upon the subject of Mr. Philip, you merely prove how nearly human ignorance of the crude masculine variety can come to the precipice of a very unsafe conclusion.

The fact that dear Adela wore sequins, says this wise lady, when she knew that Mr. Philip thought they did not do justice to her charms, and the fact that she was at pains to let him know that her afternoon at Queen's Hall had tired her so much that she now preferred salted almonds to general conversation, should make it clear to the meanest intelligence that dear Adela had a thinking part. If, as you say, proceeds our mentor, this young man was an eldest son, and his evening clothes suited him so very well—which, by the way, one rather takes for granted in Grosvenor Square—it was just as well perhaps for him to learn to come to heel at the outset, so that both dear Adela and he might be saved unnecessary trouble after Dr. Bridge had played Op. 9.

It is hard, concludes the wise lady, for human error of the crude masculine variety to go much further than yours has done, if for a moment you could allow your deluded readers to imagine that a well-born girl could treat with more than feigned indifference an educated Englishman with a comfortable private fortune. Because no well-born girl ever is indifferent to three addresses and possibly a yacht, however much she may appear to be so.

The morning following being Sunday, dear Adela kept her bed till Monday instead of going to church.

"Where is the Pain?" said Sir Wotherspoon Ogle Bart.

The rude girl snapped at him a little, although he was such a very dear old Fellah, as Windsor Cassel used to say. But he quite agreed that dining with dull people was likely to overthrow a sensitive digestion; still for the next twenty-four hours at any rate, she must take nothing in the way of nourishment but peptonized biscuits and desiccated milk.

Mr. Philip hardly missed her genial presence at St. Sepulchre's as much as he might have done perhaps. Sitting with his mother only two rows off the chancel, with his hair brushed back from his intellectual forehead, he got wrong in the responses, couldn't find the psalms appointed for the Third Sunday, got mixed most hopelessly over the order of the prayers. He allowed his mind to wander in respect of those appointed for the Royal Family; and when the Reverend Canon Fearon, robed in full canonicals and a rather ritualistic stole, came to grips with the Laws of Moses, the mind of Mr. Philip as it envisaged him, saw a golden chariot where other people saw a wooden pulpit merely, and instead of an uncovered sconce of shining silver, a diadem of chestnut curls.

Mr. Philip finally left the chancel with the good old Mater leaning on his arm. She was in need of no assistance, but it looked maternal. They took a short turn in the park to find an appetite for luncheon, but Adela wasn't among the earnest throng of morning worshipers a-walking there.

In spite of Adela's absence from the sacred function, Mr. Philip did himself quite well at luncheon, as he always made rather a point of doing in the matter of his meals. In the opinion of this natural philosopher, if you have a good inner lining the crosses of this life are easier to bear.

Adela read the *Ladies' Field* and nibbled at her biscuits and toyed with her desiccated milk. But we shall waste no sympathy upon her, she having snapped at the Court Physician—such a very dear old Fellah, with a delightful old-world manner, and a clinical thermometer in the lining of his hat.

Where Mr. Philip spent the afternoon of Sunday is not germane to the issue, but where he spent that of Monday can be handed in as evidence if the Court is quite agreeable.

At five o'clock on Monday, the heir to the barony looked in at a resort of fashion that we almost blush to mention. Youth and beauty in their various disguises were also there. Some in mink and some in ermine, some in frieze and some in velvet, some with clocks upon their wrists, some with clocks upon their stockings, some in paint and some in feathers, some in hobbles, some without 'em, some in turquoise earrings, some in pearls, some in mutch of sanguine hue, some in coalscuttle, some in beehive and other arch creations; and as east of Piccadilly the weather was really getting rather chilly, all we hope, wearing Jaeger underclothing.

Ping went the heart of the heir to the barony as each fresh arrival entered. Ping went the heart of Philip. Ping, ping it went continuous, as the patent doors revolved upon their hinges, and rank and fashion, youth and beauty swept proudly past commissionaires and other quite unimportant people. But as late as 5:15 Arminius Wingrove hadn't shown a feather.

A puss in every corner worrying buttered scones and muffins with the aid of silver-plated forks. All across the parquet, under palms and awnings, the latest things by Paquin, toyed with their real old china teacups, and coquetted with toast and bread, butter and Monsieur Eschoffier's most delightful comfit cakes.

Ping went the heart of the heir to the barony; ping went the heart of Philip; but although the strain upon that important organ was terrific, Arminius Wingrove never showed a feather.

The Blue Bulgarian Bazoukas discoursed really delightful music; tunes by Strauss and tunes by Wagner, oratorio by Monckton, masterpiece by Rubens, chic morsels by Debussy, rhapsodies by gentlemen whose names are easier to spell in Russian, the latest expression of the genius of German, things in Spanish, things in French, Elgar and Villiers Stanford, Sullivan and Dr. Parry, Leslie Stuart and the Abbé Liszt—but Arminius Wingrove never showed a feather.

Actually the hour of six had struck. With a glance of despair at the gold hunting repeater of infamous memory, the unhappy young man, for the good of the house, peremptorily ordered a glass of water and a toothpick. Already the motley throng of muffin-worriers, replete with tea and cake and music, had begun to take again to taxis, and to pair-horse vehicles, with and without cockades.

Now, what do you suppose had happened to Arminius? His excuse, when ten days later it happened to be forthcoming, was so comprehensive, that the dignity of human nature calls for a special chapter in which to unfold the same.

CHAPTER VII
IN WHICH WE DRINK TEA AGAIN AT THE CARLTON

IT was the simple fact that Arminius Wingrove had forgotten all about it. Let us not be hasty in our blame, however, since according to his *amende* to Mr. Philip at least ten days after his breach of faith, he made it clear that he was without any sort of stain.

The plain fact was, Arminius Wingrove had been commanded at a moment's notice to shoot at Burnham Beeches with Windsor Cassel. Comes as a great surprise to you, does it? Shouldn't though. Because, when Lord Grey de Stilton caught a chill on the liver through standin' on damp grass, and had to turn it up at a moment's notice under the best medical advice, who was there else to send for but England's handy man?

Poor idle rich young fellow had to chew dust and practice the complete art of humility. When next they encountered at the Betterton, ten days after this event, and the vain young man, not yet in possession of this information, ventured to reproach Arminius familiarly, by name, that most distinguished man fixed his eyeglass with his accustomed air of mental power, and as good as asked the heir to the barony, whose career at present was not, who the dev-vil he was a-talkin' to. Not in so many words, perhaps, but it almost sounded like it.

"You are a rotter—so you are—to go back on your word like that. You promised to be at the Carlton last Monday week, and you never showed a feather. And it's no use sayin' that you did, because I waited an hour and a quarter for you."

Arminius transfixed the poor unintellectual, though not with the naked eye.

"*You* haven't been to Windsor." Arminius removed his hat in his loyal mannah. "*You* don't know the Cassel."

Poor young upstart took it in the neck terrific.

"Telephone or send a wire? Only just time to pack my bag and then damn near had to have a special. I feel obliged to chastise you, you cub, for this display of eg-o-tism."

The luckless heir groveled and begged pardon. Supposed the affairs of the Empire must always take precedence of a muffin-worry, even if the fairest of her sex was going to be there. He had a Constitutional mind, you see, even if the facts of his life are all against him.

"But I'll overlook it this time," said Arminius with an air of really princely magnanimity, "if in the future you will try not to overrate yourself, and you will also promise not to be so cursed familiar in mixed company. One don't mind so much in this Bohemian resort, but when I as a dinner guest meet you as one of the mob at the Blenheims I particularly hope you will not address me as Fathead before all the congregation."

Deep shame overflowed the blonde complexion of the heir.

"You've been asking for it a long time," said Arminius grimly, "and you've got it now. Cheek I abhor from a new creation. But as I like you pooty well, I am going to forgive you."

The heir to the barony was only too glad to be forgiven on these terms by such a distinguished man; and in this, although we may lay ourselves open to correction, we consider him quite right.

He could not sleep just now, you know, when he went to bed at night. A rare vision enthralled him when he dined, and when he supped; playing at billiards under the guidance of Mr. John R-b-rts; losing at games of chance, money he had never earned; riding in the park with Adela, who had recovered of her indisposition, had been to High Cliff, and had come back again; going with his mother to concerts and museums like a dutiful young chap; buying cigarettes at Harrod's Stores; shaving in the morning with his safety razor or pulling off his socks at night—his only thought was Cinderella and her diadem of chestnut curls.

He had been several times in front to see her, but he didn't know Mr. Hollins anything like well enough to dare to go behind. And not one of his many friends in the metropolis seemed able and willing to bring him closer to his divinity, with the sole and august exception of Arminius Wingrove.

That is why perhaps the young man ate humble pie *ad. lib.*

"I've only one afternoon free this month, and that's to-morrah," said Arminius.

Most unfortunate, but it happened that on the morrow the vain young fellow was booked to take Adela and her Cousin Jane from Cumberland, to drink tea at Claridges'.

"Just as you like," said Arminius Wingrove. "My only afternoon."

The young man knitted his brow in grave perplexity.

"I wonder if I could persuade Adela to turn up the other shop and come to the Carlton. It isn't quite playing the game though, is it?—and she mustn't know what for, because if she does I'm bound to get it."

So supremely bored looked Arminius in the stress of these parochial affairs, that like a wise young fellow the heir to the barony decided to curtail them somewhat.

"Yes, I'll be there at five to-morrow, Fat—I should say Minnie. Carlton is quite as expensive as the other box, although the crush is greater. You know Adela Rocklaw, don't you?"

"Met her at High Cliff," said Arminius casual-like. "Old Warlock's daughter. Girl you are engaged to."

"Not engaged exactly."

"Thought you were."

"Not exactly. Not official yet."

"Time it was then," said Arminius, with magisterial gravity. "Just the girl for you."

Perhaps.

Life itself is a great perhaps says—no, there hardly seems sufficient provocation to fix the blame upon any private individual for his venerable saw. But all the same, *peut-être* is perhaps the most important word in any tongue.

The morrow at the hour appointed brought forth the vain young fellow with Adela looking very smart, and Cousin Jane from Cumberland looking rather the reverse of fashionable. Precautions had been taken to book a comfortable table in a sequestered angle, where the Blue Bulgarian Bazoukas would be unable to wreck any conversation that might happen to be forthcoming.

The heir was feeling all to pieces, and Adela, as usual, was not so very gay. She had said Claridges' distinctly. Why had he not obeyed instructions?

Five P. M. but never a sign of Arminius Wingrove. But even the heir to the barony, with that sinking sensation behind his waistcoat, as he ordered tea and muffins for three persons, was man of the world enough to be aware that Arminius mightn't appear very much before the hour of six had tolled. He was beginning slowly to realize that individuals so humble as himself had meekly to hoard any small portions of the loaf of human amenity that were cast upon the waters.

Indeed, the odds were six to four on that Arminius would either forget this little engagement for the second time, or that he would be again commanded to the Cassel, his keen sense of hu-mor having, according to ru-mor, made an e-nor-mous impres-sion. But even if calamity again overtook the heir to the barony it was by no means clear that he was going to grieve. For a fortnight past, asleep and awake, had he dreamed of Cinderella, but the gallant sportsman was feeling rather cheap just now, as the young minx opposite, with the cool blue eye and the chin of domination—'ware 'em, you young bachelors—was engaged in giving him tea without any sugar in it.

"What!" said the young cat.

They could hear her quite three tables away.

"A Mr. Wingrove. Says he's met you. Thought you wouldn't mind meeting him again—awful brainy feller—and he's bringin' a girl he knows."

"What!" snarled the young puss, starting on her first muffin.

Even poor Cousin Jane from Cumberland, who was nearly twice the age of the young minx, got snubbed most severely when she ventured some perfectly commonplace remark. And such a nice, sensible girl as she was.

"How do you spend your time in Cumberland?" said the unfortunate heir, beginning to feel horribly cheap, and wondering if he might venture upon a large whisky and a small apollinaris.

"I hunt otters all the mornin'!" said the nice, sensible Cousin Jane, "and in the evenin' I gen'rally knit bed-socks."

You must talk a little louder, please, now that the Blue Bulgarian Bazoukas have opened fire upon that magnificent 1812 Overture by Tchaikowski.

"How rippin' they play, don't they, Adela?" said Cousin Jane from Cumberland. "So nice and loud."

"What!" snarled the young minx above the strident outcries of the Great Retreat.

"Rather makes you think of otter huntin'—just when they begin the worry."

The irresistible *élan* of the Blue Bulgarian Bazoukas inspired Mr. Philip to an act of hardihood. Under cover of the clamor, he hailed a passing waiter.

"Large whisky and small polly," said the desperate young man.

This classic beverage within him, he was once more able to look the whole world in the eye. It was indeed a happy inspiration, for hardly had his courage risen, when at 5:27 by the hand of the clock among the greenery, a most distinguished figure emerged through a host of common persons and converged upon the scene.

Ping went the central organ of the young man's being. The hour and the man had come to hand. And ye gods, there was Cinderella!

Retain your presence of mind, my lords and gentlemen, the authentic heroine is coming to you, as fast as her feet in very sensible number threes can bring her. And her trim form is inhabiting a plain blue serge costume, made by a very ordinary provincial tailor on very reasonable terms, and her mighty sensible head is surmounted by a *hat*, not a coalscuttle, nor a sauceboat, nor a beehive, but a form of headgear well behind the fashion two years ago in Manchester; and there is just a common strip of fur round her throat, because the weather east of Piccadilly is still blowing rather chilly, and she has to sing this evening.

She is coming past the tables, whose critical occupants are wondering why young ladies from the suburbs are admitted to this Valhalla which holds all that is best and brightest in the metropolis. Not, of course, that Arminius comes within the purview of this misdirected criticism; his far-flung gaze surmounted by a noble topper, astrachan collar inches deeper than the heir's, white spats by Grant and Cockburn, and a very snappy pair of gloves.

The far-flung gaze of Arminius Wingrove has seen the vacant places at the table, although he affecteth not to notice 'em.

"How d'ye do, Lady Adela. When did you return from High Cliff?"

Rude girl slowly raised a fin.

"Awful good of you, Fat—Minnie, I mean—old boy." The heir, stronger for his liquid sustenance, spoke in tones of deep emotion. "Sit here, Miss Caspar, won't you? I know you are Miss Caspar, I've seen you so often lately."

General introductions, which even the best society seems at present unable to dispense with.

Nice, sensible Cousin Jane from Cumberland smiled so kind and pleasant, and thought they ought to have more tea.

"And what's your choice in cakes, Miss Caspar?" said the young man brightly. "Scones or muffins or some of those toppin' things with sugar on 'em."

"Thanks, anything'll do for me," said the Principal Girl, as easy as if she was playing Cinderella. "No fresh tea—quite warm and liquid. Just as I like it. I'll pour it out myself. No use offering tea to Mr. Wingrove. A whisky and apollinaris, and—I didn't catch your name—hadn't you better have another one yourself?"

Oh, how rippin'! The heir to the barony was wreathed in smiles. But the rude girl opposite stared considerable at this simple spontaneity and natural ease of bearing.

"Such a bore," said Arminius. "Got to go to-morrah to the Cassel. Daresay, Lady Adela, I shall meet you there."

"Papa is so poorly," said the rude girl, thawing some. "But, of course, Aunt Selina will explain it to the Cassel as she is in waiting there just now."

"Don't know Blackhampton?" said Cinderella. "Oh, but you ought to know; it is every Englishman's duty to know Blackhampton. Dear, dirty old Blackhampton!" said the Principal Girl. "The very best town in England. You are always *sure* of your friends in front when you play in Blackhampton."

The heir to the barony supposed it was so. Not in any perfunctory spirit. How do you suppose the young chap could be perfunctory with his divinity drinking her tea, and eating Monsieur Eschoffier's famous comfit cakes as though she enjoyed them thoroughly.

Don't let us heed the rude girl opposite. She is quite safe in the competent hands of Arminius.

"Here's your whisky and polly," said the Principal Girl; "and Mr. Wingrove's, too. Better have some more tea, I think. Miss Percival and Lady Adela are going to have some to keep me company. Oh, yes, *please*. And I say, waiter, have you any of those cakes with currants in them, like you get at Blackhampton?"

The waiter said he would inquire.

Never mind the rude girl opposite; Arminius has her in hand. With that chaste pair of yellow gloves and his knowledge of the world, he will be able to manage her, no doubt. A Miss Caspar—Drury Lane—going far said those who knew—the Backinghams were taking her up—the stock was bound to go higher. Sorry that the stage had no interest for Lady Adela.

Yes, the Cassel was looking awfully well just now, in every way quite its own bright and cheery Presence.

The heir to the barony said he had been to Blackhampton.

"Only once—but I've been there."

"Oh, how interesting!—to play for the Olympians against Blackhampton Rovers—no—really—I didn't catch your name—why who *are* you?"

"My name is Shelmerdine," said the heir to the barony, as modestly as the circumstances permitted.

"Why—*the* Mr. Shelmerdine!"

If there was such a person as *the* Mr. Shelmerdine, the heir to the barony feared it was a true bill.

Cinderella, with her provincial naïveté, didn't know that lords and people did such democratic things as these.

"Do all sorts of wild things when you are up at the 'Varsity," said the heir to the barony. "And, of course, you know, that was before my guv'nor got his leg up."

"Now it is no good your being modest, is it?" said Cinderella. "Because I know all about you. It was you who kicked those three goals against Scotland in Nineteen Four."

The confusion of the heir to the barony was dire.

"Not a bit of good your blushing, is it? I saw the match—I was only a flapper then playing Fairy Footlight at the Royal Caledonian, Glasgow, and I went with my Aunt Bessie to Celtic Park, and saw you kick three goals, and I won tons of chocolates off the Scotchies in the Company, because I had put my pinafore on old England, as I always have, and as I always shall—"

"—They say the new system of drainage at the Cassel—"

"—Steve Bloomer himself couldn't have done better than you did that day—and it is no use your being modest, is it?—"

"—And the Kaiser is one of the most charming and well informed men I have ever—"

"And so you are really the great Phil Shelmerdine, with your hair brushed just as nice as ever. Even when I was a flapper and wore a blue ribbon round my pigtail, I used to think your hair was lovely. You ought never to have left off playing socker; but I suppose you kind of had to when Mr. Vandeleur made a peer of your poor father. But England needs you more than ever now that Steve is on the shelf."

"Don't you find the theater a very trying profession, Miss Caspar?" said nice, sensible Cousin Jane from Cumberland. "Aren't the late hours a fearful strain?"

"One sort of gets used to them," said Cinderella. "I'm as strong as a pony; and it's great fun; and it is wonderful how one gets to love the British public."

"And how the British public gets to love you, Miss Caspar—not, of course, that I mean that that is wonderful."

Not so bad for a very dull young man. We only hope the young fellow won't get out of his depth, that's all.

"Oh, Homburg is the greatest bore of all." The seventh unmarried daughter suspended the story of her sorrows to train a gaze of twenty-four candle-power upon the heir.

"I shall never forget your Cinderella—and such a cold as you had! But it seems to be better now."

"The best way with a cold is to pretend you haven't got it."

"And I shall always remember the way you sang 'Arcadee,' and 'Nelson and his Gentlemen in Blue.' We were in a box, you know, second tier on the left, my friend Clapham and his five kids—lost their mother last year—and their nannas. They simply howled with joy. That little Marge is a nailer. I should like you to see her, Miss Caspar, and when she grows up she'll be just like you."

Miss Insolence opposite rose in the majesty of black velvet and white ermine.

"Goo'-by."

Arminius received a fin at an angle of sixty-five degrees.

"Jane."

Cousin Jane was so glad to have met Miss Caspar, and before she returned to Cumberland she hoped to have the pleasure of seeing her play Cinderella.

"Well, I'm awfully proud to have met you, Miss Caspar. And I hope you'll bring some of your friends along to the Albany, B4. My number on the telephone is 059 Mayfair, and I'll lay in a stock of cake."

"Delighted!—and you must come and see us, me and my old granny—Mrs. Cathcart—used to play Lady Macbeth to John Peter Kendall and those old swells, although I daresay you can hardly remember them. But she's a dear, Mr. Shelmerdine; and if you want to hear about the dignity of the profession, and how her granddaughter's lowered it, come round to Bedford Gardens, Number Ten, any Sunday afternoon, and you'll say she is the dearest old thing about."

CHAPTER VIII
IN WHICH WE MAKE THE ACQUAINTANCE OF THE GODDAUGHTER OF EDWARD BEAN

MR. PHILIP counted the hours till Sunday came. He was sorely infected now by the deadly virus.

As for those three goals against Scotland, he had clean forgotten them. They were never mentioned in his own little world. In Grosvenor Square, in particular, no store was set by such irresponsible undergraduate behavior. There his career only dated from the time he had managed to get his commission rather easily in the Second, and he had never been quite forgiven for tiring of a respectable course of life so soon.

It was strange that this sportswoman, so full of sense and pluck, had seen him in the crowded and glorious hour when life was his in its fullness. He had lived in those days, perhaps a little crudely, but now he wanted to have done with his idleness and start to live again.

He was in love with Mary Caspar, and that was all about it! Whether she drank tea at the Carlton or warbled ditties on the boards of Drury, she rang tune in every note. No wonder that she was the uncrowned queen of many a provincial city; no wonder that every errand boy in the metropolis whistled "Nelson" and "Arcadee."

On his way to his rooms he called at a news-agent's, and invested a shilling in picture-postcards of Mary Caspar.

"I suppose you sell a lot of these?"

"Hundreds," said the young man behind the counter. "We've sold out three times in a fortnight, and the demand is increasing."

On Sunday afternoon, as five o'clock was striking from St. Martin's Church, Mr. Philip drove up to Bedford Gardens and pulled the door bell of Number Ten.

A trim little parlor-maid led him up to a cozy little drawing-room.

Miss Caspar received him with unaffected cordiality.

"And this is my Granny, Mr. Shelmerdine," said Cinderella proudly.

Grandmamma was a stately old dame in a turban, turned eighty-four—a really wonderful old lady. Her speech was lively and forcible; and her manner had the grace of one who had grown old with dignity. It had a half-humorous touch of grandeur also, as of one who has known the great world from the inside, and is not inclined to rate it above its value.

Grandmamma shook hands, and said she was glad to meet the son of his father.

"A good and honorable and upright man I'm sure, Mr. Shelmerdine, although his politics are all wrong to my mind. You see, we artists, even the oldest of us, live for ideas, and these unfortunate Vandeleurites—but we won't talk politics, although it was I who bought Mr. Vandeleur his first bells and coral. At that time nobody except his mother and myself, and possibly his nurse foresaw that he was the future Prime Minister of England. Polly, my dear, the tea."

"You boastful old Granny," said Mary. "And I don't think Mr. Shelmerdine is a bit impressed."

"But I am—*awfully*," said Mr. Shelmerdine gallantly, handing the Bohea.

And he came within an ace of dropping the cup on to the hearthrug, because Miss Mary chose at that fateful moment to twitch her adorable left eyelid so artfully that the young man had to whisk away his countenance to keep from laughing in the face of Grandmamma.

"Mr. Shelmerdine, tell me, have you seen my granddaughter play at the Lane?"

Yes, Mr. Shelmerdine had, and if he might say so, admired her playing awfully.

"I am sorry to hear you say that," said Grandmamma. "To my mind she displays a strange lack of ambition. We are an old theatrical family, Mr. Shelmerdine. When I was her age I was playing Lady Macbeth to John Peter Kendall."

The young man was mightily interested, although to be sure this was the first he had heard of John Peter Kendall; but happily he had a useful sort of working knowledge that *Lady Macbeth* was the name of a thrilling drama by the author of *Money*.

Miss Mary was quite unscathed by this damaging piece of criticism.

"Yes, Granny dear, but then you had genius—and that's a thing that doesn't often occur in any family, does it?"

"Mary child"—the natural grandeur showed a little—"it is a mere *façon de parler* to speak of ambition, respect for one's calling, determination to live up to the highest that is within oneself, as genius. Moreover, the absence of genius is a poor excuse for lowering the traditions of a distinguished family. Mr. Shelmerdine, I hope you agree with me."

Appealed to at point-blank range, the young man was fain to agree with Grandmamma. But if his note of conviction was not very robust, it must be remembered that his present ambition was to run with the hare and to hunt with the hounds.

"By taking pains," said Grandmamma, "and showing a proper reverence for its calling, even a modest talent may add a cubit to its stature. That at least was the opinion of John Peter Kendall and Mr. Macready."

Mr. Shelmerdine cordially agreed with those great men.

"To think of my granddaughter playing Cinderella at the Lane when she should be playing Lady Macbeth at His Majesty's!"

"Oh, but ma'am," said the young man, "she is a nailin' good Cinderella, you know."

"A *nailing* good Cinderella, when her great-grandmother played with Garrick, and one of her forebears was in Shakespeare's own company!"

The young man thought silence would be safer here. Still, knightly conduct was undoubtedly called for.

"I hope you won't mind my sayin', ma'am," said he, "that she's the finest Cinderella I've ever—although I daresay I oughtn't to say it in her presence."

But Grandmamma would admit no extenuating circumstance. Mary was a disgrace.

"Well, dear Granny," and again that wicked left eyelid came into action, "you can't deny that next year the Lane is going to double my salary, although I am sure I get quite enough as it is."

"Child, do you suppose that John Peter Kendall would have urged such an excuse?"

Grandmamma's majesty dissolved Cinderella in light-hearted mirth.

"I quite see your point, ma'am," said the heir to the barony, playing as well as he knew how.

"Mr. Shelmerdine," said the old lady, "I make you my compliments on your good sense."

It must certainly be said for the heir to the barony that he made quite a favorable impression upon Grandmamma. Rather a plume in the bonnet of the parfit, gentil knight moreover; because as Granny had been kissed by

Mr. Dickens, used regularly to call upon Mr. Thackeray in Young Street, had dined and supped with Mr. Gladstone, and had a very poor opinion, indeed, of Mr. Disraeli, she must be reckoned rather a judge.

CHAPTER IX
A LITTLE LUNCH AT DIEUDONNÉ'S

SORE were the ravages of the ancient malady. It made it worse for the sufferer that he had never had it before.

He was twenty-eight, a very healthy and normal citizen, "a little slow in the uptake," to be sure, but with private means already, and the heir to the paternal greatness. He should, of course, like other paladins, have tried to keep out of mischief by serving his king and country.

It was a mistake to have left the Second, said his admirable parents. He wanted a wife, said all the world. It was really necessary that a young man of his age should provide himself with this most indispensable accessory.

In his torpid way he rather agreed. But he got no forrarder, although it was perfectly clear that the indispensable accessory was his for the asking.

To be sure, he had never exactly hit it off with Adela. Self-willed and overbearing young women, doubtless, had their reason to be; but he was much too shrewd a young chap to crave to be tied up for life with one of them. Still, if he wasn't careful the fetters might easily be riveted. Things had rather shaped that way for twelve months past.

All the same, it behooved him to be wary. The fruit was ripe. A single shake of the branch and it might fall from the tree.

Cinderella had shaken the tree pretty severely. Simple, kind and cheerful she was just the sort of girl you could get on with. Straight as a die, overflowing with life and sympathy, she had the noble faculty of being genuinely interested in all the world and his wife.

Would she come out to lunch?

Oh, yes, any day except Wednesday and Saturday, when she had to play.

So the very next morning they lunched at Dieudonné's, and everything seemed perilously pleasant.

Punctual to the minute! How delightful to have a table in the corner! The restaurant of all others she liked to lunch at; and lark and oyster pudding and Chablis, the fare above all others that she coveted.

Comparisons are odious, but really...!

Didn't he think Granny was wonderful? And really *quite* great in her day. A link with the past, of whom the profession was very proud.

Was Miss Caspar never tired of the theater? Wasn't it an awful grind? Didn't she ever want a night off? When she felt as cheap as she must have been feeling a fortnight ago last Saturday, didn't she just want to turn it up?

Perhaps—sometimes. But then her motto was Nelson's, never to know when you were beaten. It was Nelson's motto, wasn't it? Besides, having two thousand people in your pocket gave you such a sense of power. And then the princely salary, a hundred pounds a week, and next year it was going to be doubled. She really didn't know how she would be able to spend it.

Why spend it at all? Why not invest it at four and a half per cent.?

Oh, yes—for a rainy day!

Such an idea was evidently quite new to Cinderella, and she proclaimed it as the very zenith of human wisdom.

"You must let me spend a little, though."

She spoke as though he had charge already of her hundred pounds a week.

"Not more than a fiver now and again. No need, really. Of course when you take a holiday abroad you can dip a bit if you want."

Granny thought the provinces were vulgar, but Cinderella was quite sure that Mr. Shelmerdine didn't agree with Grandmamma.

"Now look me right in the eye, and tell me whether the provinces are vulgar. Honest Injun now!"

The good gray eyes were open to a width that was positively astonishing. "Look right in, and consider yourself upon your oath."

Mr. Shelmerdine did not agree with Grandmamma—being upon his oath.

"No, of course. The provinces are hearty and easy to get on with, and we are very fond of each other, and I don't consider either of us vulgar. It is Granny's Victorianism, to which I always pretend to give in—although I don't, of course. Do you know dear, dirty old Sheffield? The next time you go and play against the Wednesday—I beg your pardon, I had forgotten those wretched Tories had made your father a peer—well, the next time you go to Sheffield—which you never will again—ask the dear old Tykes whether they have ever seen Mary Caspar as Alice in *Dick Whittington*. Why, it was I who presented the Cup and Medals to the United when they won the Hallamshire and West Riding Charity Vase."

"Oh, really."

"You mustn't say, 'Oh, really.' You must say, 'Did you, ma lass! I wish I'd been playin' in ta match.'"

Would Miss Caspar have a cigarette?

With pleasure; but she insisted on lighting his before he was allowed to light hers.

"I wonder if I know you nearly well enough to call you Philip?" she said at about the fourth puff. "Your name is such a long one, isn't it?"

The heir to the barony was bound to admit that his name was long, and that even Philip was shorter when it became Phil.

"Wouldn't Phil be just a little familiar, considering that we have only known each other a week?"

"I seem to have known you for years and years and years."

"Well, if you really *mean* that, Philip, I don't think there is any reason why it shouldn't be Phil. But you mustn't go beyond Mary, you know. There is only one other person outside the family who calls me Polly, because somehow I object to Polly on principle. And you'll never be able to guess who that is."

"Mr. Vandeleur?"

"Dear no—of all people. I am a perfectly ferocious Rag."

"Well, I hope it isn't—?"

"—Be careful, Philip. *Very* dangerous ground. But, no, it isn't he. The only other person who is allowed to call me Polly is the Lessee and Manager of the Royal Italian Opera House, Blackhampton."

A sudden pang of consternation went through the heart of Mr. Philip. There was a confounded ring on her finger!

"Goose," said Mary, amused not a little by the course of the young man's gaze. "Old enough to be my father. But he's a dear; and if I ever marry anyone—which I never shall, of course—I don't think I should mind marrying him, although he's just celebrated his silver wedding, and he's got a family of eleven, seven girls and four boys, all with a broad enough accent to derail any tram in Blackhampton."

Yes; Mr. Philip enjoyed every moment of this little luncheon at Dieudonné's.

Before going to misspend his afternoon at one of his clubs, he accompanied the charmer as far as Bedford Gardens. They went on foot for the sake of the exercise, which she vowed she would rather die than do without; along the Strand if he didn't mind, because she loved it so.

The Strand was a wonderful place, they both agreed. Certainly, he had been in it before—often—though always on the way to the play or to supper at the Savoy. But he had to admit that this was the first time he had come to it in broad daylight as an amateur.

"You get more human nature to the square inch in the dear old Strand than any place in the world," said this young woman who had traveled the five continents in the exercise of her calling.

"Piper, miss. 'Orrible murder in the Borough."

Mary was proof against this lure, and with true feminine irrelevance proceeded to pile insult upon the head of injury by calling upon a young gentleman of nine, who apparently was not going to Eton next term, and whose person was held together by a single button, to explain the absence of his shoes and stockings.

"Aren't got none, lidy."

"Why haven't you?"

"Ain't 'ad none, lidy, since mother was put away for doin' in father a year lawst Boxin' night."

"I daresay it is quite a good reason," said Mary Caspar, "if only it could be translated into English. What did your mother do to your father?"

"'E come 'ome ravin', and mother throwed a paraffin lamp at him, and the judge give her ten years."

Mary Caspar opened her purse and produced the hundredth part of her week's salary.

"Never let me see you again without your boots—or your stockings, either."

The recipient looked at the sovereign doubtfully. Then he looked up at the donor.

"Lidy," he said, depositing this incredible wealth in some inaccessible purlieus of his late father's waistcoat, "you're a toff."

The heir to the barony was rather silent as they turned up Bedford Street. He was, of course, a drone in the hive, but he sometimes indulged in the pernicious habit of turning things over in his mind.

"There's something wrong, you know, somewhere. A kid not a day more than nine, all on his own. I think we ought to have got his name and address."

Mary thought he would have forgotten his name, and that he wouldn't have been at the trouble to possess himself of anything so superfluous as an address, but she agreed with a further display of true feminine irrelevance—and what would any Principal Girl be without it?—that they certainly ought to have got them.

And so they turned back for the purpose. But the bird had flown. They walked as far as Trafalgar Square, crossed over, and came back on the other side, but their quarry had quitted the Strand.

"We must look out for him again," said the heir to the barony. "Although I expect there are thousands like him."

"Millions," said Mary.

"And, of course, it don't matter what you do in individual cases, so the Johnnies say who know all about it—but you must let me stand that sovereign, although it is sweet of you and all that."

The heir to the barony produced the sum of one pound sterling, and inserted it in Mary's muff, a very ordinary sort of rabbit-skin affair.

Mary declined point-blank to accept the sovereign, which irresponsible behavior on her part made her escort look rather troubled and unhappy.

"Oh, but you must."

"Why?"

The heir to the barony seemed perfectly clear in his own mind that she ought to do as she was told, but not being gifted in the matter of clothing his thoughts with language, the reasons he gave seemed both vague and inadequate to an independent-minded young woman whose salary, for the time being, was equal to that of the First Lord of the Treasury.

They parted on Grandmamma's doorstep, with a hearty hand-shake, and a reluctant promise on Mary's part to come out to tea on the morrow. The young man walked on air to one of his numerous houses of call, firm in the conviction that he had never enjoyed a luncheon so much in all his born days.

"Ye-es, Agatha, I a-gree with you," said the first Baron Shelmerdine of Potterhanworth at half-past seven that evening, twisting his face in the torment of achieving the conventional without a suspicion of the baroque or the bizarre. "The ve-ry next shirts I order from Hoodlam shall all turn down. Harold Box, I believe—so why not I? Oh, confound it all—that's the third I've ruined."

"Fetch another Wally, and I will tie it for you," said the Suffolk Colthurst superbly.

It was humiliation for a Proconsul, but we are pledged to tell the truth, the whole truth, and nothing but the truth in this ingenuous narrative. And of their courtesy we ask none of our readers to accuse us of malice.

"You must bend a bit, Wally." The Suffolk Colthurst grappled firmly with the situation. "Better order two dozen at once from Heale and Binman. Theirs carry more starch."

Here it was that Destiny came into the picture, casual-like.

"Wally." The Suffolk Colthurst had just achieved a reticent self-respecting single bow. "Now that Lord Warlock has agreed to that settlement, if I were you I would send round a note to the Albany for Philip to come and see us in the morning."

"Well tied, Agatha. I'll write a note to Philip, now."

If the truth must be set down, and that, of course, is essential in all circumstances, the parental communication, in spite of the fact that it had an impressive device on the back and a motto in a dead language, was not the first note that was opened at B4 the Albany on the following morning. It was not the second or the third either, because there was quite a pile of correspondence in front of the kidneys and bacon at a quarter-past ten in the forenoon of Tuesday, the first of February.

"Dear Philip," said the parental communication when it was open at last, "your Mother will be pleased if you will come to luncheon to-morrow, as there is an important matter she would like me to speak to you about. Luncheon at one-thirty sharp, as I have to go down to the House. Your affectionate Father, S. of P."

Mr. Philip helped himself pensively, but not illiberally, to kidneys and bacon. He sprinkled salt and pepper over them, spread mustard on the plate, buttered his toast, poured out a cup of tea of almost immoral strength, read over the parental communication again, and then made use of an objurgation.

"I wish the good old Mater wouldn't get so meddlin'," said he.

Nevertheless, like a dutiful young man, he decided he must go and lunch at No. 88 Grosvenor Square. But by the time he had put on his boots with five buttons, had been inserted into the coat with the astrachan collar, and had sauntered forth to his favorite florist's, twirling his whanghee cane, somehow the good old sky of London didn't look quite so bright as it did yesterday.

His favorite florist's was in the charge of his favorite young lady assistant, Miss Pearson by name, whom a fortnight ago he had serious thoughts of calling Sally without her permission. But a good deal of water had flowed under London Bridge in the meantime, so that now whether she gave her permission, or whether she withheld it, he no longer yearned to be guilty of any such freedom.

Still, Miss Pearson was a very good sort for all that, and the heir to the barony raised his hat to her this morning in his politest manner, although perhaps it is right to remark that he would have done so on any other morning, and even if Miss Pearson had not been such a very good sort—but in that case he might have gone a little higher up the street, as far as Miss Jackson.

"Mornin', Miss Pearson. How are we?"

Miss Pearson was so-so. Had been to the Coliseum to see *Richard III* the previous evening.

"Have you been to Drury yet, Miss Pearson?"

No, but Miss Pearson's best boy had promised to take her next Monday—Monday being her night out.

"I *envy* you, Miss Pearson," said the heir to the barony with emotion. "And the young chap—of course."

"Mr. Shelmerdine," said Miss Pearson, "do you know what my impression is?"

Mr. Shelmerdine had not the faintest notion what Miss Pearson's impression was.

"My impression, Mr. Shelmerdine," said Miss Pearson, "is that you are in love."

No rebutting evidence being put in, Miss Pearson grew grave and serious as became a young lady of good Scottish lineage on the spindle side.

"If you'll take my advice, Mr. Shelmerdine, you'll go a short sea voyage. I've noticed a deterioration in you during the last fortnight. It is far worse than when Cassie Smallpiece was at the Gaiety. I shall go and see for myself on Monday, but I've no opinion of actresses as a class. It is time you married that Lady Adela, you know."

It was the first time that Miss Pearson had been moved to these communications as far as this particular client was concerned; but the fair president of the smartest florist in Piccadilly was a lady of considerable social insight.

"Well, Miss Pearson," said the heir to the barony, slowly and thoughtfully, "you know that I always value your opinion, but Mary Caspar is an absolute nailer."

"Go across to Dean and Dawson's," said Miss Pearson. "Or you can use my telephone if you don't want to run the risk of crossing the street. Egypt or Switzerland, or a short sea voyage. Think what a blow it would be to your father if you didn't marry a lady in society."

"Ha, you haven't seen her yet, Miss Pearson," cried the incredible young man. "If I could book a couple of stalls for Monday, do you think your young chap would mind accepting 'em?"

"Only too pleased, I'm sure," said Miss Pearson promptly. "No false delicacy about Alf. He's in the greengrocery the other side the Marble Arch."

The heir to the barony was a little "slow in the uptake," but, like others who labor under that natural defect, in the end he generally contrived to get to his destination.

"I hope you ain't throwin' yourself away, Miss Pearson," said the heir to the barony. "Blow to your people, I'm sure, if you are side-tracked by anything under a bank clerk."

"Money before position, Mr. Shelmerdine, is my motto," said Miss Pearson. "If you've got the one, you can always get the other."

The heir of the barony seemed rather impressed by this pearl of wisdom. He pondered it while that very able and personable young woman twined a piece of wire round a posy of violets. And then, as if to prove a general proposition, Position itself appeared, and somewhat abruptly terminated this instructive *tête-à-tête*.

Position entered in the person of a youthful marquis, leading a bull terrier whose natural beauty was almost as chastened as his own.

"Why, Shel—haven't seen you for years!"

Position held out a hand, gloved somewhat aggressively in yellow. His senior by four years shook the gauntlet warily.

"Mornin', Sally."

Position turned its back and put its elbows on the counter. It might have been the sole proprietor, not only of those most desirable lock-up basement premises, but of Miss Pearson and all its other contents. Still, no reproof was forthcoming.

During an even earlier phase of Position's adolescence, it had been Mr. Shelmerdine's privilege as a member of the Eleven, a member of Pop, and of other high dignities, to lay into Position in no uncertain manner. Alas that his zeal had proved so unfruitful!

Autres temps, autres mœurs. Had we the pen of the sage, the fervor of the poet, the *sæva indignatio* of the preacher, what a theme is here, my lords and gentlemen! Position not only usurping the badge of intimacy, reserved for the peers of the Keeper of the Field, but actually venturing to take *pas* of him, addressing Miss Pearson by her first name, setting his elbows on the counter, and removing a bunch of violets from her ample bosom, while he—the unspeakable humiliation of it—actually had to wait meekly for his own.

Had there been a toasting fork within the precincts of those desirable lock-up basement premises, it is appalling to think of the consequences that might have ensued.

Miss Pearson handed Mr. Shelmerdine his bunch of violets in a manner sufficiently *dégagé,* as though her interest in him had assumed a less acute phase. Raging within, the heir to the barony, a mere 1905 creation, sought the purer air of the Ritz Arcade, leaving the field to 1720, who could be heard saluting Sally not too chastely, as his early benefactor hurriedly crossed the threshold of his favorite florist's, and came into somewhat forcible collision with an elderly, but ample lady from Missouri, who was on a visit to Europe, and who had come to stay at the Ritz Hotel.

The elderly ample lady from Missouri was fluent in her diction; the heir to the barony was abject in his apologies; but eventually the incident was closed by the unlucky young man escorting the American citizeness to her palatial temporary residence, and giving her into the care of the hall porter.

Evidently, it was not going to be his day. But let justice be done to the Fates, even when they are behaving just about as badly as they know how. Had it not been that the heir to the barony lingered a moment to exchange a few brief but urbane civilities with the hall porter of the Ritz, he must inevitably have walked into Adela and her Pa who were passing very slowly and impressively by the portals of this coign of the plutocracy.

It was a hair's-breadth escape. The young man had only just time to realize his danger, bolt across the road, almost under the very wheels of an oncoming Barnes and Hammersmith omnibus, escape a threefold death by violence at the instance of the passing motor, board a taxi, and in a voice tense with emotion beseech to be driven to Romano's.

A gin and vermouth might be said to have saved this full but chequered life.

"Called me Shel—my God! If only I'd got that long-handled, old-fashioned one with the five prongs—!"

CHAPTER X
AFFAIRS OF STATE

STILL feeling rather a puppet in the hands of Fate, Mr. Philip reached No. 88 Grosvenor Square, the corner house, about twenty minutes after the hour appointed. But as the great Proconsul really must be at the House of Lords by a quarter to four, luncheon had already begun.

"I notice, Philip," said S. of P., who had arranged with the Woolsack to address his fellow peers in support of the Daylight Saving Bill that afternoon, "that you hardly realize the importance of the part played by time in the lives of us all. I said half-past one distinctly in my note."

The unfortunate young man apologized very humbly and politely to the great Proconsul.

Considering what an Odyssey his life had been that morning, the young fellow made a very decent luncheon. Just the wing of a woodcock, and a bit off the breast, a few slices of York ham, a jam puff or so, a bite of cheese and an imperial pint of bitter ale out of a presentation silver tankard bearing the arms of Ch: Ch. Blind instinct seemed to tell the young man that he must keep up his strength, since there was a dull sensation behind the chocolate waistcoat, knitted for him by his mother, which clearly suggested that trouble was looming in the middle distance. Port wine, Green Chartreuse, a big cigar, and black coffee all played their manly parts. Yes, with the help of the gods he might be able to keep up his end all right; although he was by no means sure that he liked that concentrated, governing-classes look in the eye of the good old Mater.

The after-luncheon conference in the library was most impressive. The Governing Classes were distinctly fortissimo; and in spite of his ample sustenance, Mr. Philip felt rather meager in the presence of this deep reverence for the established order, and so much of that which is best in the public and private life of these islands.

Lord Warlock, subject to certain contingencies, was prepared to accept other contingencies in respect of Adela. The First Baron was admirably clear and statesmanlike in his *aperçu* of the most interesting position which had been evolved by the higher diplomacy.

"Sometime in October, at dear Saint George's," thought the good old Mater.

The heir to the barony was silent, dismal, and undone. He had hesitated about a second Green Chartreuse; he wished now that he had obeyed his inward monitor. There was a sense of vacuum behind the knitted chocolate waistcoat that was really the devil.

"It is like this, you know—" The young man floundered and came down rather awkwardly at fence Number One. "Adela and I—well, fact is, we haven't—"

The Governing Classes showed great patience.

"We haven't sort of—you know—?"

"I am afraid we don't, my boy," said S. of P. with the blandness that goes so well with conscious power.

"The end of October is such a *good* time," said Mother, "especially if there is to be an autumn session."

"Oh, yes," said the young man, "but, fact is, Adela and I have never quite hit it off from the start."

The Governing Classes, with lowered eyelids, looked at one another across the chaste expanse of Messrs. Maple's hearthrug. The pause was rather trying. Yes, an awful pity about that second Green Chartreuse.

At last S. of P. was sorry.

This may look a little inadequate on the part of S. of P. But it wasn't really. Eton and Balliol, "distinguished public service," terms of intimacy with His Majesty's late Government are not incapable of resonance on the domestic hearth. It was already clear that the higher statesmanship might have to be tempered with a little benevolent autocracy.

"Warlock is really most liberal—that is, of course, for an Irish peerage."

"*Most* liberal, Wally," the Suffolk Colthurst chimed.

"Isn't October rather soon, Mater?" said Mr. Philip, beginning to shape like a tailor, at fence Number Two.

"The sooner, the better, we think."

"I agree with you, Agatha."

"Oh, but—" said the unfortunate heir.

The Governing Classes were to be butted no *buts*, however.

"Philip," said the good old Mater, "your father has been at the trouble to draw up an announcement for the *Morning Post*. It will be shown to Lord

Warlock this evening, and with his sanction it will be sent to the editor by the first post to-morrow."

"I don't think I should trouble, Mater, if I were you," said the unhappy young man.

Now, that really was rather ineffectual, and sounded quite as much so as it appears.

"I think the announcement should be made at once," said Father. "Adela is a charming girl; you are a very lucky fellow; and you are to be envied. Philip, my dear boy, I congratulate you with all my heart."

S. of P. shook the heir to the barony warmly by the hand.

"Kiss me, dear Philip." And Mother offered the blonde, bland frontispiece.

No seaworthy excuse can be put forward for dear Philip's refusal to kiss his mother. Not a refusal exactly; but he burked the issue by asking to be allowed to read the announcement which had been drawn up for the *Morning Post*.

A very little research discovered the interesting document on Father's writing-table.

Mr. Philip read the announcement as duly set forth in the elegant maternal hand. He then sighed heavily; and then it was the Green Chartreuse at last began to play up to its reputation.

The young man folded up the announcement carefully, and placed it in his cigar case.

"Well, if you prefer to send it yourself—so long as it *is* sent, my dear boy."

"I hope you won't forget all about it, Philip," said the maternal one.

"But I am not going to send it," said the young man, all sweetness and simplicity.

Yes, pretty good work by the Green Chartreuse.

Dead silence.

Mother got the first gun into action.

Why wasn't dear Philip going to send it?

Dear Philip thought it was premature.

Mournful interlude on the tragic note. Warlock would not take kindly to delay, said Father in deep tones. Was it kind to dear Adela? asked the third person at the conference.

"I shall be glad to hear the grounds of your objection," said S. of P.

It was merely that they didn't seem quite to hit it off. Adela was an awfully nice girl; the fault was his entirely; but still he didn't quite feel as if—

In this charming passage in the aria the Suffolk Colthurst fluted tremulously. So *sweet* a girl as Adela, so *good* a family, such *excellent* connections—

The great Proconsul was rather grieved, in his deepest and richest baritone.

But there it was! said the Green Chartreuse, doing its level best for England, Home and Beauty.

Nevertheless, the Governing Classes seemed hardly able to concede that it was there. They were dining that evening in Mount Street to meet Warlock's sister, Dumbarton's sixth duchess. Hadn't dear Philip better return the sheet of note paper to his father?

The young man rose slowly to confront the Governing Classes.

"Fact is, you know," said he, "I haven't asked her yet; and if I did ask her I'm pretty certain she wouldn't have me. Not that I blame her, of course."

"Philip, you must listen to me," said the Proconsul. "Lady Adela will, as I have reason to know, be quite willing to identify herself with the wishes of her family. My dear boy, allow me to express the hope that you, as the future head of yours, will show yourself equally amenable."

The firmness of the Powers was stupendous. But firmness comes easy when you have passed your life thinking imperially.

Wasn't it all rather selfish of Philip?

Has a man a right to be selfish, even when he's staking his life's happiness? Depends on the sort of man you are, said the Green Chartreuse. Personally, we consider, said the Green Chartreuse, you will be the "absolute it" in the fool class if you allow your people to queer your pitch for you on the score of Family. Adela is a cat, and you know it; Mary Caspar is a girl in a million, and you know that, too; you have no need to be ambitious; you will have quite as much money, and quite as much position as is good for any young fellow. If you don't want to make a clean sweep of all the prizes in the Juggins Department you will answer in the negative in a quiet, firm, and manly voice.

Here it was, moreover, that Destiny, who seemed to hold a watching brief for the defendant, played a very useful card for the Green Chartreuse. S. of P. consulted his watch, and raised his well-brushed white eyebrows in dismay. A quarter past three already; and he made a point of never missing prayers if he had to keep an appointment with the Woolsack.

In the circumstances, there was only one thing to be done; it was to move that the Conference stand adjourned.

"Come to luncheon on Sunday, Philip, and in the meantime there is no need to send the announcement to the papers."

We hope you concur, my lords and gentlemen, that it was a decidedly useful card that the old fox, Destiny, had played for the Green Chartreuse.

CHAPTER XI
LICENTIOUS BEHAVIOR OF THE GREEN CHARTREUSE

THE heir to the barony was a dull young man—it is idle to pretend that he wasn't—yet in his slow-witted way he had a habit of turning things over in his mind. If he married Adela it would give pleasure to his excellent parents; it would advance him in the eyes of the world; people would say here is a young man with more in him than we thought—see how well he has married. But there was no shirking the fact that if he married Adela he was bound to be miserable for the rest of his days.

Weak, disgraceful thoughts, Shelmerdine, quoth the Twin Brethren, Eton and Christ Church. It was not on *our* playing fields you learned to be so puerile. No girl in London makes a more distinguished appearance in black velvet. You will shoot at High Cliff. With what grace and charm will the seventh *married* daughter preside over that dear little house in Grosvenor Street, on the left, going to the park, which your admirable parents have promised her admirable parent to take for you on a lease, in order that you may both be near them. Shelmerdine, we don't know when we have been so ashamed of an alumnus of ours. If you haven't enough character, sir, to tackle the very ordinary job of driving a young woman on the curb—as every young woman ought to be driven for her soul's welfare at the beginning—you are a miserable shirker, sir, and unworthy of your liberal nurture.

Sir, in that event, we wash our hands of you; and you are free to form an alliance with this underbred Bohemian—it is not our custom to mince our language when our emotions are deeply stirred! You will bring down the gray hairs of your admirable parents in sorrow to the grave; your portrait will receive the freedom of the gutter press; you will never be asked to shoot at High Cliff; you will bring tragedy into your own life and into the life of others—in fact, sir, and in a word—one understood these infernal safety-razors were guaranteed not to cut gashes into one's neck!

Little recked Cinderella of the reason why the heir to the barony had to appear at tea-time on Friday done up in court plaster. He was also strangely pensive and embarrassed.

She was as gay and as charming as usual; and she had just been engaged to create the title rôle in Mr. Wingrove's brilliant new play at the Millennium, that was to be produced in the middle of Lent. But poor Philip was far from being himself. Still, he insisted on walking home with her to Bedford Gardens.

However, by the time they had reached the Strand, that romantic thoroughfare, the murder was pretty well out. It really came out at the moment they stood on the edge of the kerb opposite Charing Cross, waiting to commit their frail lives to the maëlstrom of mechanically propelled vehicles.

"Fact is, old girl,"—the heir to the barony gripped Mary firmly by the arm to see that she didn't step off the kerb too soon—"fact is, old girl, I want a pal. Will you be a pal to me?"

"Why, of course I will, Philip," said Mary, as they walked arm in arm into the jaws of a Barnes and Hammersmith 'bus.

"A pal for life, I mean, old girl."

By the time they had reached the opposite kerb, Mary was quivering. And the color in her face surmounted the natural pallor of her profession.

"Oh!—but, Philip—"

"You *will*, old girl!"

"I don't think that Granny—besides—!"

"Besides what, old girl?" The knitted chocolate waistcoat was being grievously assaulted.

"It wouldn't do—for you, I mean—although it is sweet of you to have asked me, Philip."

"It's whether it would do for you, old girl. I'm not much of a chap, I know, but I should begin to pick up a bit—I'm sure I should—if I had got a real pal like you to pull my socks up for me."

"It isn't because I don't like you, Philip," said Mary, so nicely that the owner of the knitted chocolate waistcoat wanted to clasp her to it in one of London's most important thoroughfares. "It is because I do."

"Won't you risk it, anyway?"

"But I don't think I ought—really. Your people, you know. And I'm sure that Granny—"

"Oh, but this is our affair. I've thought it all out; and if a chap wants a wife, I don't see that anybody has a right to meddle. It's askin' a lot, I know—your career and all that—but I've enough for two, and you wouldn't have to sing and dance to three thousand people when you were feeling so cheap you didn't know how."

Mary was troubled by this importunity as a girl as nice as she was bound to be. She had already grown to like this rather heavy young man. She felt capable of being a father, a mother, a brother and a sister to him, or any equally near relation whose function it would be to pull his socks up for him. But she was also a very sensible and unselfish girl, moreover, a pretty clear-sighted one; and when she said that Granny would never, she really meant what she said, and a great deal more than she did say.

All the same, she was very proud and happy as she turned up Bedford Street, with the hand of Philip still gripping her arm very tightly, although in this haven there was not a solitary Barnes and Hammersmith 'bus to warrant a continuance of such a course of behaviour.

The heir to the barony, in our humble judgment, was about the luckiest young fellow in London just then to be walking up Bedford Street with a girl as good as gold in his possession. Very nearly, but not quite in his possession. He had come at his fence so boldly; it was an inspiration to have taken off just where he did in the welter of Barnes and Hammersmith omnibuses in front of Charing Cross; his solid, manly British qualities had shone out suddenly so clear and free, that where another might have hesitated and come a purler, this sportsman had gone straight at the obstacle and very nearly come home a winner. Very nearly captured the queen of beauty, but not quite, although she was feeling very proud and happy because of the honor done to her—and it *is* an honor, O you young ladies of Newnham and Girton, the highest that can be paid to you, so please to remember, my dears, when you turn down your thumbs to the next undesirable—and she blushed so charmingly all the way up the street that it was a pity there were not more lamps in Long Acre by which you could have seen her.

Their feet swayed together in a delightful rhythm, in their radiant progress: spats by Grant and Cockburn, and Mr. Moykopf's most superior hand-stitched russia leather, and eight and eleven penny Walk-easies made by the gross at Kettering, which had no spats upon 'em. Yes, it was a lovely walk in the dark amid the purlieus of Long Acre. Several times they lost their way, and didn't try very hard to find it. And then, suddenly, from out the distant mirk, where the time-spirit was keeping its grim eye upon 'em, the hour was tolled from Saint Martin's Church.

One—two—three—four—five—six—seven!—the excited heart of the Principal Girl counted each stroke. Cinderella must fly. She would only just have time to drink her Oxo, and to get into her rags—which were not rags at all really—and fix her war paint, if the great British public was not to receive one of the severest disappointments in its annals.

"Well, think about it, old girl—although I don't mean to take 'No.' I've made up my mind to that."

They were on Granny's doorstep now. And there let us leave them without waiting to see what happened.

Did something happen?

There is no need to gratify idle curiosity upon the subject.

The really important thing that did happen, before Cinderella slipped her latch-key in the door, was that Mr. Philip re-affirmed his manly determination not to take "No" for an answer. He vowed, moreover, that he would come and interview Grandmamma after she had had her siesta on the afternoon of the Sabbath Day.

CHAPTER XII
THE PROCONSULAR TOUCH

IT had been a crowded and glorious week for the Green Chartreuse, but it was not until the Sabbath Day that it had really to embrace the crisis of its fate. Mary had not said "Yes," and she had not said "No," but she had seemed to imply that Grandmamma might prove obdurate. Then there was also that little obstacle in Grosvenor Square to negotiate. Yes, taking one fact with another, it was reasonably clear to the Twin Brethren that Sunday promised to be a rather important day in the calendar.

The heir to the barony did not go to church on the morning of the fateful day, although, perhaps, it would have been wise to have done so. He read *The Referee* instead, in order to collect a few ideas as to his general bearing in the convention after lunch in the library at No. 88.

The Governing Classes were decidedly FF. Not a day later than the third week in October, Warlock thought, otherwise it would play the dickens with his shooting.

"Egypt would be such a *nice* place in which to spend the honeymoon," said Mother.

Little recked the Powers, however, of the Homeric struggle that was being waged within the precincts of the immaculate braided morning coat that sat so perfectly upon the manly form of Mr. Philip.

Do if you Dare, said the Twin Brethren.

Don't be a Cur, said the Green Chartreuse.

And as no young man likes to be thought a Cur by a boon companion, the miserable yet half-exultant Philip gathered his forces for the conflict.

"There's something, Father, I'd like to say," said he, as he performed the superfluous action of tucking the end of his handkerchief still further up his shirt-sleeve.

Perfect frankness was invited.

"I would like to say," said the young man, "that I don't feel that I can marry Adela."

The timepiece with the silver tones had the only speaking part for the space of ninety seconds. And then out spoke Mother.

"Phil-ipp!"

"Can't—possibly—Mater."

"Phil-ipp!"

And all this time the benevolent autocrat, who had put on his eyeglasses and taken them off again, and then put them on again, was trying to recapture the touch of a great Proconsul who had started out in life with a Balliol scholarship.

"Of course, my dear boy, *you* must decide." The Proconsular eyelids conveyed delicately to the Suffolk Colthurst that, after all, the *Suaviter in Modo* cannot be surpassed in the hands of an acknowledged master. "But, as Warlock knows already, we shall be very happy to make Lady Adela welcome in the family."

"Oh, yes, of course, but you see—"

Neither parent appeared to see, unfortunately. The poor Green Chartreuse grew desperate.

"So you see, I've kind of proposed to another girl."

The Proconsul took off his eyeglasses and buttoned his coat; the Colthurst of Suffolk manipulated her third and fourth chins into a condition of majestically eloquent inarticulation. The silver timepiece alone was moved to make an observation, and that, of course, was quite irrelevant.

"Her name is Mary Caspar, and she is an absolute nailer," said the heir to the barony.

"An actress, I believe," said Mother, who, like every member of her family, had an almost uncanny memory for names.

"An absolute nailer," said Mr. Philip.

Three weeks ago the young man had taken to Jaeger underclothing, but even that hardly seemed able to cope with the thermometer.

"It isn't exactly definite. She seems to think there are things against it, but I'm going to talk it over this afternoon with her old grandmother."

"Who, pray, is her grandmother?"

"Her name is Mrs. Cathcart, and she lives at 10 Bedford Gardens."

"I will call upon her," said Mother, somewhat ostentatiously, making a note of the address.

"Philip," said the great Proconsul, "you must listen to me. I am afraid this is all very irregular. A man of your age, my dear boy, ought to know that in these days they give swingeing damages for breach. This must go no further, you understand; and the best thing we can hope for is, that the young woman's grandmother is as sensible as we have a right to expect an old woman and a grandmother to be."

"But I am goin' to marry Mary if she'll have me, father," said Mr. Philip, all politeness and simplicity.

Fortiter in Re, as classical scholars do not require to be told, is the natural corollary of *Suaviter in Modo*. Spasmodic trumpetings were emitted freely by the great Proconsul. The Colthurst of Suffolk also had recourse to the clarion note. It was really a scene of great majesty and power, and it lasted until hard upon tea-time. The behavior of the heir was subversive of all there was left to subvert in the Cosmos, since the wicked Welsh Chancellor's deadly missiles had knocked Mars and Jupiter and several other leading planets clean out of their orbits.

What would People say? said Mother.

Swingeing damages these days and rightly, re-affirmed the great Proconsul.

"She wasn't that sort of girl at all," said Philip the manful. He had had to make all the running. Father and Mother mustn't misjudge her. And they must forgive him if he seemed to have lost his head a bit, but it was all for the best, he was sure. Never been able to hit it off with Adela; hadn't any tastes in common. It would be better so.

"Don't be absurd, Philip," said Mother, upon G sharp.

Was it conceivable that the eldest son was without a sense of moral responsibility? blandly inquired the ex-Resident of Barataria North-West.

"I hope the grandmother of the person is a woman of the world," said Mother. "I will call upon her without delay."

And then the heir to the barony spoke like a very nice young chap. He sincerely hoped his excellent parents would not blame him more than they felt obliged. He had thought it all out in the watches of the night; it would be all for the best, she was such an absolute dear. He would be awfully pleased to trot her round for inspection; and was there really any reason why a man rising thirty, with a private income, should not marry the nicest girl in London?

"But, then," said Mother, "dearest Adela is a girl in a thousand."

"And please don't forget," said Father the Proconsul, "you are my successor."

If only he could Abdicate! murmured the wretched Green Chartreuse.

Neither Father nor Mother heard it, fortunately.

And then in tones of solemn music, the silver-tongued timepiece chimed the hour of half-past four.

"By Jove," said the heir to the barony, with a sigh of relief. "How awfully late!" And rising to his full height from Messrs. Maple's choice upholstery, he dispensed a cloud of sweet and gentle and perfectly sincere apology.

He did not desire to bring a moment of pain to his excellent parents. He was sure it would be all for the best if only he could persuade her to have him—he had not persuaded her yet, worse luck! But, in spite of this charming urbanity, Mother took no leave of him; and Father had "a damned disinheriting countenance," as he escaped through the door of the library.

A pretty mess you have made of things, you fool, snarled the Twin Brethren, as Joseph showed him over the door-mat and whistled up a taxi.

CHAPTER XIII
JANE'S AFTERNOON OUT

THE Green Chartreuse was able to break its journey at Romano's, as it passed that home of wassail *en route* to Bedford Gardens. And having done so, it was able to answer back a bit, but only in a very minor key just now, my lords and gentlemen.

The dear girl herself opened the door to Mr. Philip; it was Jane's afternoon out. Wasn't Mary very tired after the two performances yesterday? Not a bit. But wasn't he a bit below the weather? No? She thought he looked so, rather. Merely because he had been lunching with his people, was it? Very wrong to make a joke of such a filial action, particularly as Grosvenor Square on a Sunday is thought to be the home of the serious.

Granny was sitting very upright in the cozy corner, and looking very stately in her smartest cap with lace on it, that had been worn by Siddons. An approximation of the grand manner when she shook hands. The weather was not cold, perhaps, for the season of the year; but when one was turned four-and-eighty, one's vitality was perhaps a little less than formerly.

Miss Mary brought in the tea, looking frightfully demure.

Grandmamma herself had a preference for Chayney tea. She hoped Mr. Shelmerdine did not object to Chayney tea; if he did, there was whisky and soda which some gentlemen preferred. John Peter Kendall always preferred it; likewise John his father; and she had heard that this preference was shared by Edward Bean, who was her godpapa—and the silver mug he gave her at her christening was upon the chiffonnier.

Had Mr. Shelmerdine heard that the Lane was going to double Mary's salary, and desired her to sign a contract for a term of five years?

"Two hundred a week, Mr. Shelmerdine. A fabulous sum. Why, I don't think that Garrick—"

"Not a penny more than she deserves, ma'am," averred the heir to the barony.

"Mr. Shelmerdine, it is enough to make Edward Bean turn in his grave. A preposterous sum for a girl of very ordinary ability, without any true histrionic genius. Why, I don't think that Siddons in the heyday of her power—"

"Why, of course she didn't, you jealous old Granny. And if I were a woman of genius like you are, and she was, I shouldn't be getting it either and signing contracts. Don't you agree, Philip?"

And Miss Mary fixed the young man with her glorious gray eye, and said to him quite distinctly by the Marconi system: "Say Yes, in your heartiest voice, like a dear boy."

So of course, the young fellow had to say Yes, when he meant No.

It is unkind to make comparisons, but tea and cake in Bedford Gardens, thought Mr. Philip, is a far more interesting function than a four-course luncheon farther west. And yet the young man had by no means a great appetite just now. It was the crisis of his fate. Had Mary told Grandmamma? And what would Grandmamma say, if told she had been? For men and gods these were all-important questions.

Certainly, the old thing in the real lace that had been worn by Siddons was very *grande dame* indeed. Diction clear cut, lively and forcible; not a single English actor worthy of the name in the present generation, and she hadn't seen the foreign ones; in fact, the race had perished with Mr. Macready, who had taken her to Gadshill to drink tea with Mr. Dickens.

"But, what about Sir Henry Irving, Granny?" said Mary, covertly twitching her charming left eyelid at the heir.

"Pretty well, for an amateur, my dear, but better fitted to play the hind-leg of a dragon than the Prince of Denmark."

"Oh, how terribly severe!" said Mary, so demurely that the Morning Coat had an overpowering desire to clasp her to its braided bosom.

"Good at melodrama no doubt, my dear," said Grandmamma, "in the Surrey theaters; but to my mind wholly unfitted to carry on the great tradition of Edward Bean and John Kendall."

It is by no means clear that the Braided Morning Coat was able to enjoy Grandmamma's caustic criticism of the present hopelessly inferior histrionic age as much as it might have done, because there was that sinking sensation somewhere about the third button which somehow seemed to suggest that it was going to be its turn presently. And although a very ordinary sort of coat, which put forth no special claim to be endowed with the gift of prophecy, in this it was not a great way off the mark.

When at last its turn came, it seemed to arrive rather suddenly. It was when the Chayney tea and the cake and bread-and-butter, having ceased to have attractions, were removed by Mary, still acting as deputy to Jane the parlor-maid.

"Mr. Shelmerdine," said the Lady Macbeth to John Peter Kendall, "I am given to understand that you have been kind enough to make my granddaughter a proposal of marriage?"

"I hope you don't mind, ma'am," murmured the Braided Morning Coat, whose diction, however, although that of Eton and Ch: Ch:, was for the time being, at any rate, nothing like so distinguished as that of Grandmamma.

"I may say at once, Mr. Shelmerdine," said the Lady Macbeth to John Peter Kendall, "that I am sensible of the honor that has been paid to my granddaughter. Further, I may say that she also is sensible of the honor that has been paid her, as every right-minded girl should be, even when, as in this case, she is unfortunately unable to avail herself of it."

That unhappy sense of inadequacy was coming upon Mr. Philip which afflicted him on the occasions he called at the Foreign Office to look up the friends of his youth.

"Mr. Shelmerdine, you are a personable and mannerly young man—I am old enough to speak with freedom, and even if I were not I have always been accustomed to use it. You have considerable private means, my granddaughter informs me, and I think it is probable that you will make an excellent husband for a young woman in your own sphere of life; but, to be quite frank with you, Mr. Shelmerdine, I do not feel that I can give my consent to the match."

The Braided Morning Coat was cast down not a little.

Still, Grandmamma knew how to temper firmness of character with kindness and consideration; and that, of course, the world has a right to look for in majestic old ladies who have played Lady Macbeth to John Peter Kendall.

"My granddaughter, Mr. Shelmerdine, comes of a very old theatrical stock. One of her forebears—an ancestor of my own—played in Shakespeare's own company. Without impropriety, I think I am entitled to say that her standing in her profession is likely to be one of eminence."

Braided Morning Coat hardly needed that assurance.

"In the circumstances, Mr. Shelmerdine, perhaps I am entitled to ask what your own profession is, and the nature of your standing in it?"

This question was a little too complex for the Braided Morning Coat to be able to answer offhand. Still, the admirable garment struggled manfully, and did its level best.

Four years in the Guards, but at a loose end at present. Had thought of going into Parliament. Lady Macbeth allowed that the ablest young men in the country made rather a point of finding their way into Parliament, and long might it be so; but unfortunately, this particular able young man was not in Parliament yet.

"If it will help things, ma'am," said the Braided Morning Coat, "I will see about it at once."

It was spoken like a man of spirit and an English gentleman, which after all is just what you expect of a Braided Morning Coat and Spats by Grant and Cockburn; but Grandmamma, confessing to reluctance, was bound to say that, although this spirited conduct might help things a little, she was afraid it would not help them sufficiently.

Braided Morning Coat was awfully sorry. So was Grandmamma, sincerely sorry. Such a mannerly and personable young man; same school as John Peter Kendall, though not the same college. But it appeared to her, speaking with all reserve, and an ample sense of responsibility, that Mr. Shelmerdine's status in his profession—whatever his profession might be, and she was not so clear on that point as she would like to be—was due to the fact that he was the eldest son of his father.

Braided Morning Coat confessed frankly that it might be so, although he was not without pecuniary resources of his own. There was also a small property in Cheshire which had come to him recently through his Aunt Tabitha, and was let on a five years' lease to one of the founders of the Zionist movement.

"I learn from my granddaughter, Mr. Shelmerdine, that your father is a Peer."

Braided Morning Coat humbly made that damaging admission.

"And that you succeed to the title?"

Braided Morning Coat, beginning to feel very low and miserable, pleaded guilty to this also.

"All this, to my mind, Mr. Shelmerdine, constitutes an insuperable barrier." Diction beautifully clear and mellow. How can it be otherwise with the Bean and Kendall tradition!

"Let me make myself quite understood, Mr. Shelmerdine. It hardly seems right, to my mind, that an old theatrical family should form an alliance with a comparatively recent peerage. I believe, Mr. Shelmerdine, 'comparatively recent' is not in excess of the facts. Jane, my parlor maid, has looked it up in *Debrett*, as my eyesight is not of the best. Created 1904, I believe, to the best of my recollection, during Mr. Vandeleur's second administration."

The answer was in the affirmative.

"Your father is a man of great distinction, I understand, a Proconsul who has rendered invaluable service to the Empire. All that I have heard about him redounds to his honor, but I cannot think he would give his sanction to this proposed alliance. I may say that I should not, if I were he."

Braided Morning Coat was rather distressed.

"The fact is, Mr. Shelmerdine, I am strongly opposed to this modern craze for contracting matrimonial alliances between the theatrical profession and the peerage. To my mind, they are two entirely alien institutions. They both have their personal traditions and their private status, of which they have a right to be jealous; but it seems to me, and I am sure I voice the opinion of John Peter Kendall, were he not in his grave, that this unfortunate custom, which has lately come into vogue, lowers the dignity of both those institutions, is demoralizing in itself, and tends to diminish the respect in which either is held by the Public."

Braided Morning Coat felt that "Hear, hear!" would have been appropriate to this beautifully delivered oration. But it had not the spirit now to say "Hear, hear" to anything. Its fond but presumptuous hopes lay shattered in a thousand pieces.

"The Public expects certain things of you, Mr. Shelmerdine, as the future head of a distinguished family. As a woman of extended public experience, I would like to give you this piece of advice, which was given to me by Mr. Macready: Never disappoint the Public, and the Public will never disappoint you. You have your duties to fulfil—to yourself, to your family, and to your country. I do not say that my granddaughter would be incapable of helping you to fulfil them, because a member of an old theatrical family, in my judgment, Mr. Shelmerdine, is unworthy of the great traditions in which she has been bred if she cannot adorn any position to which it may please Providence to call her. But, at the same time, I recognize that public opinion looks to you to form an alliance elsewhere. I am sure it will be a great disappointment to the world, and a great grief to your excellent parents, whom I have not the pleasure of knowing, but who, I am sure, must be very worthy as well as very distinguished people, if you should persist in this desire to form an alliance with my granddaughter."

Braided Morning Coat, for all the compliments paid to it, which it had every reason to think sincere, began to feel as chastened as if it had been knocked down and run over by a Barnes and Hammersmith omnibus.

Long before Grandmamma had said her say, the unlucky garment hadn't a kick left in it.

Where was Mary? Somehow it did not seem to be playing quite fair to leave him all this time to the tender mercies of Grandmamma. Full of mischief like the rest of 'em, thought the Braided Morning Coat. She knows all the time we are gettin' it terrific; but instead of standin' by us like a man and a brother, she retires to the basement to help Cook peel the potatoes for supper.

"I hope, ma'am," said the miserable varlet, "your decision is not a final one."

"I am afraid, Mr. Shelmerdine, that I can find no reason at present to think otherwise."

"Well, ma'am, it's hardly my fault that I may have to succeed my father."

"Mr. Shelmerdine, I quite accept that statement."

In the neck again, you silly blighter, snarled the Twin Brethren.

"I'd abdicate if I could, but I can't, ma'am, accordin' to the rules of the Constitution. My Governor says—"

"Mr. Shelmerdine, I fully appreciate the insurmountable nature of the barrier."

"I shall have enough to keep a wife, ma'am, but if you feel that I ought to go into Parliament, I shall be only too pleased to see about it at once."

Lady Macbeth appreciated the honorable nature of the proposal, which intensified her great regret. But even a seat in Parliament could not gloss over the fact that he was the son of his father.

Suddenly, the front door bell pealed loudly down in the basement and reverberated throughout the house. A casual caller—perhaps Grandmamma's old friend, Sir Swire, who called to see her most Sundays when he was in London.

The Braided Morning Coat winged a pious apostrophe to its private, particular gods.

Alas! the luckless garment was a trifle premature in its hymn of thanksgiving.

CHAPTER XIV
IN WHICH MARY QUALIFIES FOR THE RÔLE OF THE BAD GIRL OF THE FAMILY

NOW who do you suppose it was, my lords and gentlemen, who pulled that blessed bell-wire? No, not the ex-lessee of the Cornmarket Theater. Miss Mary, helping Cook to peel the potatoes down in the basement, made herself acquainted with that fact when she pulled aside the window curtains and looked up through the area. Cockades and things were before the door of No. 10 Bedford Gardens; a raking pair of chestnuts; and a smart rubber-tired vehicle with armorial bearings.

The Bad Girl of the Family, peering through the kitchen curtains, with a half-peeled potato in one hand, and a bone-hafted knife in the other, saw Jeames de la Pluche, Esquire, who in that charming but absurd fur cape reminded her not a little of Harry Merino as the Cat in the moral drama of *Dick Whittington*, leap down from his perch with marked agility, whisk open the door, and lend assistance to something very uncommon in the way of distinction.

Uncommon Distinction was blonde and bland of countenance and *very* grande dame, as you could tell by her Carriage. Looked through her folders, and saw Number 10 over the fanlight; and as this she did, one of those terrible flashes of feminine intuition overtook Mary, that this must surely be Mother.

Yes, Mother undoubtedly. Had not Philip himself the same bland, blonde frontispiece; the same ample look of nourishment; the same air of deliberation as of one a little slow in the uptake; the same faint far-off suggestion of a finely grown vegetable? And to the quick eye of the feminine observer through the kitchen curtains, there were certain things pertaining to Mother which, up to the present, Son had not developed.

The clang of the front door bell reverberated through the basement.

"Drat it, Miss Mary," said Cook. "And me not dressed yet. Would you mind letting in Sir Swire?"

"Why, of course," said Miss Mary.

"But hadn't you better leave your knife and your pertater, Miss Mary?"

"Oh, Sir Swire won't mind those, Hannah; they'll amuse him," said the Bad Girl of the Family, who was half-way up the kitchen stairs already.

Mother upon the doorstep, in her new ermine tippet, was shocked not a little, deep down in the recesses of her nature. Still of course she was far too well found in the ways of the world to give her feelings publication. But if one is so ill-advised as to visit in Bohemian circles in the afternoon of the Sabbath Day, one must be prepared for all contingencies. Still, a half-pared potato, a sack-cloth apron, and a bone-hafted kitchen knife is a rather informal reception of a real peeress from Grosvenor Square on the part of Bedford Gardens.

"Mrs. Cathcart at home?" said Grosvenor Square, No. 88, the corner house, very bland and splendid.

"Oh, yes—*won't* you come in?" said the Bad Girl winningly.

Impressive entrance of Governing Classes into an ill-lit but fairly spacious interior, which had a bust of Edward Bean over the hatstand, and John Peter Kendall as Richard II by—not after—Maclise over the dining-room door.

"Lady Shelmerdine," said the bland and splendid one, as Mary pushed the front door to with her foot because her hands were occupied.

"Of Potterhanworth?" said the Bad Girl in tones warm and velvety.

"Oh, yes," said the Governing Classes, pained, perhaps, a little.

"Philip's mother—so delighted—hope you don't object to potatoes—it's Jane's afternoon out."

But no further communication was forthcoming from the Governing Classes all the way up the solid length of stair-carpet to Grandmamma's withdrawing-room.

Mary preceded No. 88 Grosvenor Square, potato, bone-hafted knife, sacking-cloth apron and all, into the stately presence of the cap-with-lace-which-had-been-worn-by-Siddons.

"Lady Shelmerdine of Potterhanworth, Granny."

The Bad Girl turned and fled; very nearly impaled herself on the bone-hafted knife by counting fourteen stairs instead of thirteen, and continuing her course headlong until she fell howling into the arms of Cook. But in Edward Bean's goddaughter's withdrawing-room it was no laughing matter, my lords and gentlemen, we feel bound to tell you that. And we are forced to agree, though very reluctantly, with what Grandmamma said privately to the Bad Girl afterwards, which was that she would be none the worse for a good whipping.

"Mrs. Cathcart, I presume?" said No. 88 Grosvenor Square, very bland and splendid, although the tones had no need to be so icy—they hadn't, really.

"You have the advantage of me," said the Lady Macbeth to John Peter Kendall, offering her venerable hand to the angle of 1851, the Exhibition Year. "Ah, yes, Lady Shelmerdine—delighted to make your acquaintance."

What of the Braided Morning Coat, you ask, while all this was toward? Perspiring freely in every pore and leaning up against the chimney-piece, and looking rather gray about the gills.

Should it make a bolt, or should it stay and grapple with the music? The pusillanimity of the former course, tempting no doubt to a weak resolution, would involve death and damnation; but the heroism of the latter required all that could be mustered by the playing fields of Eton and Christ Church. But while the unhappy inhabitant of the Braided Morning Coat was surrendered to this problem, the stern, uncompromising eye of Mother decided the question.

"Phil-ipp!"

"Ma-ter!" And then, of course, the Twin Brethren called out the reserves. "Mrs. Cathcart—My Mother."

The bow of Grosvenor Square, No. 88, the corner house, was aloof decidedly; the bow of the Lady Macbeth to John Peter Kendall was so full of conscious power and accumulated dignity that it was really quite gracious.

"Pray be seated, Lady Shelmerdine."

Beautiful elocution on the part of the goddaughter of Edward Bean.

Lady Shelmerdine seated herself rather superbly, and opened fire with her tortoise-shell folders.

The cap-with-lace-that-had-been-worn-by-Siddons touched the electric button at its elbow.

Entrance of the Bad Girl of the Family, without her apron this time, and divested also of the potato and the bone-hafted knife.

"Mary, child, my spectacles."

The Bad Girl dived desperately in the inmost recesses of the chiffonnier; found Grandmamma's spectacles, and prepared to withdraw in something of a hurry. But she was detained.

"Has Jane returned, child?"

"Yes, Granny."

"Ask her to have the goodness to bring some tea for Lady Shelmerdine."

"Oh, not for me, thank you."

"You are *quite* sure?"

No. 88 Grosvenor Square, the corner house, was quite, quite sure. Exit the Bad Girl of the Family without daring to look once in the direction of the Braided Morning Coat that was still leaning up forlornly against the chimney-piece.

"Mrs. Cathcart," said the Governing Classes, getting the first gun in action, "I have done myself the honor of calling upon you—"

"The honor, madam, is entirely mine," Edward Bean's goddaughter assured her.

"—because of a most unfortunate state of affairs which has just been brought to my notice."

The goddaughter of Edward Bean looked sympathetic, although it doesn't always do to judge by appearances, you know.

"My unfortunate son—Phil-ipp, perhaps you will be good enough to sit down, as it is most desirable that you should follow what I say with the closest attention—my unfortunate son, to the grief of his father, Lord Shelmerdine, has made a proposal of marriage to your niece."

Lady Macbeth suggested mildly that granddaughter might be more in accordance with the facts of the case.

"Granddaughter—I beg your pardon. One has no need to tell *you*, Mrs. Cathcart, who, I am sure, are a woman of the world, that this act of my son's has caused concern in his family."

Lady Macbeth was sorry if that was the case.

"In point of fact, for some little time past my son has been engaged to Lady Adela Rocklaw."

"Not quite that, you know, Mater," murmured the unhappy Braided Morning Coat.

"—To Lady Adela Rocklaw, a daughter of Lord Warlock, and his conduct will cause pain, although, of course, madam, it has not yet become public property, and I sincerely hope it may not become so."

"You ain't puttin' it quite fair, are you, Mater?" ventured the Braided Morning Coat.

"Phil-ipp, please!" A wave of a she-proconsular hand. "Allow *me* to deal with the facts. A most embarrassing situation, madam, for two families."

"One moment, Lady Shelmerdine," said Lady Macbeth. "May I ask this question? Do I understand your son to be actually *engaged* to Lady Adela Rocklaw?"

"Yes, madam, you may take that to be so."

"Mr. Shelmerdine," said the Queen of Tragedy, "I must ask you for an explana-tion."

Braided Morning Coat, notwithstanding that it was feeling completely undone, unbuttoned itself nervously.

"The Mater's a bit mixed, ma'am, and that's the truth. I am not engaged to Lady Adela."

"Perhaps, Phil-ipp, not officially."

"No, Mater, and not unofficially, and—" Herculean effort by the Green Chartreuse—"I don't mind sayin', I've no intention—"

"Phil-ipp!"

"Lady Shelmerdine," said the Queen of Tragedy, "the situation is not altogether clear to my mind. Either your son is engaged to marry Lady Adela Rocklaw, or he is not."

"He is morally engaged to her."

"I am sorry I am unable to appreciate the distinction. Do I understand that your son is engaged to Lady Adela?"

"No, ma'am, I'm not," said the Braided Morning Coat with honorable boldness.

"But Phil-ipp!"

"It's the truth, Mater. Mrs. Cathcart asks a plain question, and there's a plain answer. And after all, I'm the chap—"

"Quite so, Mr. Shelmerdine," said Lady Macbeth, looking almost as wise as the Lord Chief Justice of England as he sits in the Court of Appeal. "This is your affair. You have a right to know your own mind—moreover, you have a right to express it."

The Braided Morning Coat felt the stronger for this well-timed assistance. It was easy to see from which side of the family Miss Mary had inherited her strong, good sense. A masterful old thing, but she really was helpin' a lame dog over a stile, wasn't she?

Blonder and blander grew the Colthurst of Suffolk. It really looked as though it might be a pretty set-to.

"Perhaps Phil-ipp, if you looked into your club for an hour—"

The Green Chartreuse, the horrid coward, wanted to quit the stricken field prematurely. But if he had, as sure as Fate, Mother would have won quite easily. Happily he did not. Mr. Philip stuck to his guns like a Briton, and Grandmamma at least thought none the worse of him for it. The Lady Macbeth to John Peter Kendall had an opinion of her own on nearly every subject; and the order of which the Braided Morning Coat would one day be an ornament had in her judgment to carry a rather serious penalty; but the old thing in her shrewd old heart—an imperious old thing, too—who had kept pretty good company for eighty-four years or so, was not altogether inclined to accept all the world and his wife at their surface valuation.

"The Family, madam," said the Colthurst of Suffolk, "is unable to countenance an alliance between my unfortunate son and your granddaughter, who, one is given to understand, is at present engaged in a pantomime. I am, however, empowered by Lord Shelmerdine to offer reparation if such is required."

These were not the actual words used by Mother. Her style was easier, a little less florid, a trifle more conversational; but manner is said to be more eloquent than matter in the higher diplomacy; thus the foregoing represents more or less accurately the ultimatum of the Governing Classes.

Grandmamma didn't look pleased; at least not very. The Florid Person was evidently taking herself rather seriously. Let her Beware—that was all—quoth Conscious Strength, amid the inner convolutions of the cap-of-real-lace-that-had-been-worn-by-Siddons.

"It appears to me, Lady Shelmerdine," said the goddaughter of Edward Bean, "that this is perhaps a matter for your son and my granddaughter, and that no practical purpose will be served by third and fourth parties discussing it—except, perhaps, in a spirit purely academic."

In a spirit purely academic! Well done, Peggy, whispered the delighted shade of John Peter Kendall, hovering somewhere in a cornice of the ceiling, immediately above the bust of himself.

"Mrs. Cathcart, as a woman of the world, and as one who is in a position to appreciate the feelings of a mother, I am sure I shall not appeal to you in vain."

When in doubt, saith the Diplomatist's Handbook, *Suaviter in Modo* is a card you should always play. But how often has Grandmamma seen it, in the course of her eighty-four summers, do you suppose?

It was here that the Braided Morning Coat felt it was up to it to say something, and forthwith proceeded to do so.

"I agree with you, ma'am," said he. "It's just a matter for Mary and me. She won't say Yes, and I won't take No, and there we are at present. But I'm goin' to ask her again, because I love her and all that, and I know I'm not worthy of her—but I'm goin' to try to be, and I'm goin' to see about Parliament at once."

The silence was ominous.

"That appears to be a perfectly manly and straightforward course to take, Mr. Shelmerdine," said Grandmamma, breaking the silence rather grimly.

Please observe that she didn't tell Mother that she declined to sanction the match. In the circumstances, therefore, it is hardly kind to blame Mother for making quite a number of errors.

Of course error the first was to come when Mr. Philip was present in *propria persona*. But that, we are afraid, was due to the aboriginal defect of a parent in underrating the importance of its offspring. What she ought to have done really, was to have come not as an important unit of the Governing Classes, but to have crept in by stealth, as it were, as the poor human mother humbly craving assistance; and she ought to have kept her foot on the soft pedal throughout the whole of the concerto.

Alas! the manner of Mother's coming had been otherwise. And the longer she remained, the less she ought to have said in order to realize the estimate she had formed of her own wisdom—and when the spouse of a great Proconsul is thinking imperially you can have no idea how great that estimate is.

"Lord Shelmerdine empowers me to offer all reasonable reparation."

Grandmamma was interested to hear that in spite of the fact that the whole matter was so purely academic.

"If there is any special form the young lady—I haven't the pleasure of the name of your niece, madam—would desire the reparation to assume, Lord Shelmerdine's solicitor will be happy to call upon her to-morrow."

"Oh, but Mater—I say—"

Slight display of *Fortiter* in order to cope with this unfilial interruption.

"It is your father's wish, Philip."

The ears of Grandmamma had seemed to cock a little at the mention of Lord Shelmerdine's solicitor.

"Forgive me, madam, if I appear dense," said the most perfect elocution.

Underplay a bit, Peggy my dear, like Fanny does in genuine light comedy, said the Distinguished Shade, smiling benevolently down from the cornice.

But this was the goddaughter of Bean, which perhaps the Shade had forgotten.

"You are talkin' rot, aren't you, Mater?" said the Braided Morning Coat in vibrant tones.

"It is your father's wish, Phil-ipp. He desires that no injustice—If thought desirable, reparation may assume a pecuniary—"

"You are talkin' rot though, Mater, ain't you?"

Incredible hardihood certainly on the part of the Braided Morning Coat. But eminently honorable to that chequered garment, perhaps the world is entitled to think.

Lady Macbeth was not looking so very amenable just now. A very masterful old thing in her way, and had always been so. And really, Mother was a little crude in places, wasn't she?

Still, we are bound to do Mother the justice that she was not aware of the fact. Indeed to her it seemed that the higher diplomacy was really doing very well indeed. Everything so pleasant, so agreeable; iron hand in velvet glove, but used so lightly that Bohemian Circles were hardly conscious of its presence. Mother was getting on famous in her own opinion, and she ought to have known.

Matrimony quite out of the question, of course, between the granddaughter of Lady Macbeth and eldest son of the House. The Governing Classes hoped that that had been made quite clear to the wife of the Thane of Cawdor.

The Wife of the Thane appeared to think it had been.

"Of a pecuniary character, I think you said?" said the goddaughter of Edward Bean.

"Yes, pecuniary; Lord Shelmerdine has no reason to think that Phil-ipp has been so unwise as to enter into a formal engagement, but it is his desire to be quite fair, even to be generous."

Steady, Cavalry! whispered the Distinguished Shade in the ear of Peggy.

"Or even generous, madam! One would be happy to have an idea of the shape Lord Shelmerdine's generosity might assume."

The unhappy Braided Morning Coat regretted exceedingly that it could not disclaim responsibility for both parents.

"But, Mater—!"

"No, do not interrupt, dear Phil-ipp. This is all *so* important and so delicate. Lord Shelmerdine thinks five hundred pounds—and I am empowered—"

And then it was that Mother found Trouble.

Trouble came to Mother quite unexpected, like a bolt from the blue—or like a shot out of a cannon, according to the subsequent version of an eye-witness.

It would hardly be kind to describe the scene in detail. Lady Macbeth, in spite of her eighty-four summers, made rather short work of Mother. Not that Mother was overborne by Christian meekness altogether. Assured Social Position, knowing itself to be absolutely right, and acting all for the best, does not always offer the other cheek with perfect facility.

Please do not misunderstand us. It was hardly a scene. The proprieties were observed with really Victorian rigidity; it was all *very* grande dame; but one being Lady Macbeth to John Peter Kendall, and the other a leading Constitutional hostess who had recently moved to Grosvenor Square, well—

Far from Mother's intention to offer an affront to the granddaughter of Lady Macbeth. But Miss Footlight of the Frivolity had quite recently received the sum of ten thousand pounds from the people of young Lord Footle, which sum was of course excessive, as dear Justice Brusher had said to Mother at dinner last evening.

"Madam, I hold no opinion of Justice Brusher; Miss Footlight I don't know, and Lord Footle I don't desire to know; but it is impossible for my granddaughter, a member of an old theatrical family, to pocket this insult."

And Grandmamma rang the bell with tremendous dignity.

Jane the parlor-maid it was who appeared this time, looking all the prettier for her afternoon out.

"Jane," said the acknowledged Queen of Tragedy, "pray conduct Lady Shelmerdine to her carriage—and in future I do not receive her."

Poor old Mother! And in her new ermine tippet, too.

"Phil-ipp, accompany me."

Philip accompanied Mother down the stairs, past the bust of Bean in the front hall, down the nine steps of Number Ten Bedford Gardens, and handed her into her carriage.

"We dine at eight this evening, Philip. Your father will expect you."

"Impossible, Mater. Dinin' at the Old Players' Club."

To give the Governing Classes their due, they certainly made exit in pretty good style from Bohemia. As for Mr. Philip, he returned to the front hall to retrieve his hat and his coat with the astrachan collar and other belongings, and wondered if it would be wise to say good-by to Grandmamma, and decided that perhaps he had better not risk it. But before he could get into his famous garment, the Bad Girl of the Family descended upon him from the basement—we are not quite sure how she managed to do it, but simple little feats in elementary acrobatics are always possible to a pantomime performer—and haled the young man by main force into what she called her Private Piggery, which in reality was a small back parlor of sorts in an indescribable state of confusion.

Having brought the froward young man to this undesirable bourn, the Bad Girl turned up the electric light, and then without any warning proceeded to fall into a state that bordered upon tears and general collapse.

The heir to the barony was not feeling so very amused just now, though.

"My opinion you were listening, you cat."

"Granny—the dreadful old spitfire!"

"Tactless of the Mater I'll admit. Quite well meant though, Polly."

"How dare you call me Polly after all that has happened!" And the youngest member of the old theatrical family whisked away her tears with a rather smart lace-broidered handkerchief, and looked almost as fierce as the Cat in the moral drama of *Dick Whittington*.

"Howlin' blunder, I'll admit; but you aren't crabbed about it, are you, old girl?"

"Please don't admit anything, Mr. Shelmerdine—and how dare you call me old girl after what has happened? Don't let me have to ring for Jane and not receive you in future—"

"So you *were* listening, you cat!"

"Wouldn't you have been—Phil-ipp?"

"It is a horrid mix-up though, isn't it? Look here, old girl, I really think the best thing we can do is to go and get married to-morrow mornin' before the Registrar."

Cinderella seemed to think, however, that such a proposal was not in the plane of practical politics.

"I know, old girl, that a Church is considered a bit more respectable; but I thought that the Registrar would be quicker and easier."

"You are rather taking it for granted, aren't you, Philip, that I'm going to marry you, when you know I'm not."

"Well, I do think, Polly, after all that has happened—!"

But somehow Polly didn't quite see it in that way. She couldn't think of such a thing without the consent of Granny. And even if Granny did consent—which, of course, her consent would never be given, his people would never give theirs, would they? so that even that would not make their prospects any rosier.

"But I thought you were goin' to be a pal to me, Polly!"

"So I am, Phil-ipp, but I mustn't marry you, must I, against the wishes of your People."

It was hard for a young man of inexperience to know exactly how much was meant by the Bad Girl of the Family when she was in this kind of humor. But whatever doubts that were in his mind, he suddenly laid hold of her quite firmly and kissed her quite soundly, and, strictly between ourselves, you young bachelors of Cam and Isis, that was just about the best thing he could have done in the circumstances.

Nevertheless the young man was still involved pretty deeply in the crisis of his fate. Bliss unspeakable was so nearly within his grasp, and yet it was so elusive. He was not without the rudiments of determination, and he had fully made up his mind that this was the girl for him, but just now he really didn't quite know how he was to enter his kingdom.

Decidedly he must pluck this peach, and he must pluck it immediately. But how?—that was the problem, with the Fates having loaded the dice.

CHAPTER XV
IN WHICH WE SIT AT THE FEET OF GAMALIEL

ON the morrow, or about midnight that same day, to be precise, when Arminius Wingrove came into the club after attending an important *première*, the great man was engaged in conversation by Mr. Philip while they dallied with devilled kidneys and other comestibles.

"Minnie," said the vain young fellow, "everybody says you are the cleverest chap in London, so I want your advice."

Rather cool, perhaps, to demand advice of the cleverest chap in London in this point-blank manner, but Arminius, who kept a generous heart beneath his waistcoat of white piqué, showed no displeasure.

"If you mean about the girl you are making a fool of yourself over," said the great man, "*don't*, is the advice I shall have to give you."

"Oh, but I've got beyond that already," said the vain young fellow with a rather grand simplicity.

"Have you, though?" said Arminius, pensive-like.

"Yes, I'm goin' to marry her if she'll have me, but the trouble is, she won't."

"Won't she, though!" said Arminius, looking rather like the statuette of himself by Sir W. G-sc-mbe J-hn.

"No, she won't, Minnie, and that's all about it, until her old grandmother gives her consent; and the old lady simply won't hear of it."

"Who is her old grandmother?" inquired Arminius, "and why won't she?"

"Her grandmother is Mrs. Cathcart, who played Lady Macbeth with David Garrick, and she's taken a prejudice against me because I'm the son of a peer."

The manner of Arminius seemed to imply that old Mrs. Cathcart had been guilty of a very unfeminine proceeding. But being a disciple of Talleyrand, the great man did not clothe his thoughts with words.

"And to make matters worse, Minnie, there was a simply frightful turn-up between her grandmother and my Mater yesterday afternoon."

With the flair of a playwright whom Hannibal had himself approved, Arminius Wingrove asked for further information.

"Simply gorgeous, Minnie, for a chap who hadn't to be in it. Wouldn't have missed it for worlds—except that I kind of wasn't in a position to enjoy it, was I? But it hasn't half crabbed the piece! Tragedy Queen ordered Mater out of the house, and says she shan't receive her in future. So it's all up with my people, and I'm afraid it's all up with hers; and the girl isn't going to marry me without the consent of all parties."

The statement of the vain young fellow seemed both florid and ingenuous to Arminius Wingrove, who had hardly been so much amused by anything since the revival of *The Importance of Being Earnest*.

"And so you don't think she'll marry you, do you, my son?"

Arminius Wingrove had not a mercenary nature, but he wouldn't mind laying a "pony" on the event. The heart of the heir to the barony gave a bound.

"Why, what reason have you to think so, Minnie?" he said in a voice of tense emotion.

"Because there's not half a reason why she shouldn't, my lad."

"But she is simply devoted to her old grandmother."

"The old lady has all her faculties, I presume?"

"My Mater thinks so, anyway."

"Well, then, there's not half a reason why the girl shouldn't marry you."

Still the reasoning of Arminius Wingrove was not altogether clear to the heir to the barony, who, to be sure, was somewhat slow in the uptake.

"Do you suppose, young feller, that any girl's grandmother would stand in the way of forty thousand a year and a peerage?"

The young man shook his head.

"No, Minnie! She's not that sort of girl; and she's not that sort of grandmother. It is the confounded peerage that has crabbed the piece."

Polite incredulity on the part of the audience.

"Minnie, old boy, everybody says you are the cleverest chap in London, but you don't know Mary Caspar."

Arminius Wingrove knew something about Woman, though.

No, ladies—not a cynical ruffian altogether. His heart was in the right place even though he took this mercantile view. Therefore, by the time the Welsh rarebit arrived the great man conceived it to be his duty to dispense something extra superior in the way of advice.

"Young Shelmerdine," said he, "what the dooce do you want to go foolin' around the stage door at all for? A chap like you ought to marry Adela Rocklaw. Make things unpleasant at home. No longer be welcomed in the best houses. Bored to tears about the second week of the honeymoon. Opportunities squandered. Much better have stayed in the Second, and gone racing quietly than to have come into money and to have broken out in this way. Now take the advice of a friend; and let us see you at the Church of Paul or of Peter at an early date awaiting the arrival of old Warlock's seventh and most attractive daughter, and I will have my hat ironed, and be proud to accompany you down the nave of the cathedral."

It was not often that this man of the world was moved in this way; but he had just staged a rattling good comedy, and devilled kidneys and Welsh rarebits and tankards of strong ale are rather stimulating diet, when you sit listening to the chimes at midnight. It is a disconcerting psychological fact, though, that no young man has ever heeded the voice of wisdom in these circumstances.

"It is awful good of you, Minnie, to take the trouble to advise me, but I'm goin' to marry Mary Caspar if flesh and blood can manage it."

"Then it's a walk-over for flesh and blood, you silly young fool," said Arminius Wingrove with rather brutal frankness.

CHAPTER XVI
IN WHICH THE MOUNTAIN COMES TO MAHOMET

MR. PHILIP found an imperious mandate from Grosvenor Square had been laid beside his silver cigar-box when he returned to the Albany at a quarter past two by the morning. It ran:—

"Dear Philip,—Your father desires to see you most particularly upon important business at ten o'clock to-morrow morning.

"Your loving Mother."

"She means this mornin', and I shan't be up if I don't go to bed soon," said the heir to the barony, sitting down before the remains of the fire to consider the situation in all its bearings.

The melancholy consequence was that not all the King's horses and not all the King's men, including the young man's body servant, were able to wake him until a few minutes before eleven, in spite of the fact that a special messenger had been round from the Home Department.

If, however, Mahomet declines to move, it is time for the Mountain to be up and doing. Therefore, just as Mr. Philip, enveloped in a sky-blue dressing-gown, was pouring out his coffee with an uncertain hand, something rather portentous was ushered into the presence of the wicked young prodigal.

The white eyebrows of the great Proconsul were a triumph of brushwork; the set of the tie was stern uncommonly; indeed, the whole paternal aspect was enough to strike awe in the heart of the beholder.

The evidence that it did so, however, is not altogether conclusive.

The young waster buttering his toast at a quarter-past eleven in a sky-blue dressing-gown, rose and offered his hand in an easy and leisurely, but withal in a manly and unaffected fashion.

"I was just comin' round, father," said the young man.

Father declined a cup of coffee and a cigarette without any effervescence of gratitude.

"Take a pew, won't you?" said the young man, returning to his toast and butter.

Cool and off-handed young fellow, perhaps, thus to receive a great Proconsul, still his tone was not without deference, even if his air was casual.

Father took a pew.

"You don't look very comfy in that one. Take the one with the arms to it."

"Do quite well, thanks," said Father, in a deep bass voice.

A state of armed neutrality?—ye-es, it did seem rather like it. Father didn't seem quite to know where to begin: Son knew better than to provide assistance.

"See in the paper that Van rather got across old Balsquith last night?" said Son conversationally.

Father had heard the debate from the Peers' Gallery.

Son wondered what would win the Coronation Vase—havin' forgotten that Father didn't go racin'.

"Philip," said Father, in tones of deep emotion, "it seems to me that you—" And Father paused.

—Are going to the Devil as fast as you can, is really what your distinguished parent desires to say to you, but he is trying to say it without treading on your feelings, which is more consideration than you deserve, you blighter!—thus the Twin Brethren for the personal information of the Green Chartreuse.

No business of his if I am, was the very unfilial rejoinder of the latter.

"Philip," said Father, after a pause, "your mother is very upset."

Young fellow was sorry to hear it—very, but the weather is always so full of surprises in February.

Mother had not yet recovered, it appeared, from the most painful scene last Sunday afternoon with the grandmother of the Person.

As the occurrence had been reported to the great Proconsul, the Person's venerable relative had not behaved as nicely as she might have done.

Son was awfully cut up about it, but he didn't quite agree. With all respect to Mother, he could not help thinking that Miss Caspar's venerable relative had been in receipt of provocation.

White eyebrows erected themselves archwise.

"But we won't go into That," said Father.

Perhaps it would be better not, said the Green Chartreuse in an aside to Messrs. Crosse and Blackwell's marmalade.

Very disagreeable, though, thought Father, and very serious, too. There was nothing more painful to a right-thinking parent than to see a son—and an Eldest Son, too—making hay of his prospects.

Didn't quite agree again with his father. The Green Chartreuse was suffering evidently from an attack of valor this morning.

"But there are the facts, my dear boy. Let them be looked in the face."

"I wish, father, you would consent to meet Mary. She's an absolute nailer, you know."

Father was so disconcerted by the behavior of Son that he kind of began to clothe his thoughts with language. A singularly unfortunate entanglement; people would be shocked; family interests would suffer; such unions never turned out well—how could they? Besides, Warlock was so sensitive. In fact, with all the conviction of which he was capable—and a Proconsul is capable of a good deal—Father urged Son to pause and reflect.

Son had already done so.

Was it conceivable?

Oh, yes, quite, if Father didn't mind his saying so. He had a private income, and she was the nicest girl in London; an opinion, he was sure, in which Father was bound to concur, when he'd seen her.

But...!!

Yes, but people were getting so much broader-minded, weren't they?

Father had heard that that was the case; but in his opinion excess of breadth was an even more serious menace to the Empire—being a great Proconsul, of course, Father always thought Imperially—than to err a little on the other side.

If you looked at things in that way, thought Mr. Philip.

Don't cheek your father and a proconsul, too, you young bounder, said the Twin Brethren.

Don't let those eyebrows overawe you, my son, said the Green Chartreuse.

How else could one look at things? the Proconsul inquired in tones of pained expostulation.

"This is the way I look at things, father," said Mr. Philip, "if you don't mind my goin' into details."

"Pray do so, my boy. I shall welcome them."

"Well, this is my feelin' on the subject. You are sort of shot here, don't you know, without anybody askin' you whether you wanted to come. You are sort of dumped here, don't you know, and told to make the best of a pretty bad mix-up. Well, I don't mind tellin' you, father, I've been gettin' rather fed up with the whole Affair lately."

An idle and selfish course of life leads invariably to that state of mind, said Father in effect, though his language was politer. It was a great mistake ever to have left the Second.

Son had got just as fed up there, though. It seemed such a silly arrangement for grown men of five-and-twenty.

Father was pained at This.

"Fact is," said the Green Chartreuse, who was a veritable Swaggering Companion this morning, "a chap is bound to get fed up unless he can find a real nice girl to take him on, and give him an interest in things. And I reckon I've found her, although I haven't persuaded her yet; but, father, if you'll be so kind as to go and talk to her grandmother, a real good sort who has played Bean with Lady Macbeth, and put in a word for me, I'm sure it would straighten things out a bit."

Father was constrained to remark at this point that he was afraid the Eldest Son of the House was hopeless. It was truly unfortunate that he could not be brought to realize the gravity of the issue.

Mr. Philip seemed willing to concede that from one point of view it would be quite right to marry Adela. But suppose you were not built in that way?

Father, however, found not the least difficulty in making a rejoinder. "Marry Adela, my dear boy, whatever way you are built in, and you will never regret it. You will have done your duty in a manner becoming to the sphere to which it has pleased Providence to call you. Your mother will be pleased; I propose to double your present income; Warlock is prepared to be generous in regard to Adela's settlement; I am sure High Cliff will view the arrangement favorably; the little house in Grosvenor Street can be had on a short lease on reasonable terms; Mr. Vandeleur is inclined to think it would do no harm to the Party; most agreeable, accomplished, and charming girl; what could any young fellow—but why labor the point?"

Son rather agreed that it might be taken as read.

Still the fact remained that if you are not built in that way you are bound to be up against it.

The Proconsul had no pity for such weakness of fiber, such general infirmity of character.

"Do you suppose, my dear boy, that when I married your dear mother I had no qualms?"

It may have been that this important truth was wrung from the great Proconsul before he realized its imminence. It was a period of considerable emotional stress just now, you must please remember.

"Do you suppose I did not realize that my life was not going to be altogether a bed of roses at first? But I am proud to say I was ambitious, and I can look all the world in the face and say I have never regretted my action. Our life together has been exceedingly harmonious; your mother is a most estimable and a thoroughly *good* woman; and I should have been guilty of the greatest error of my career had I allowed any infirmity of purpose to frustrate a union which has been so abundantly blessed by heaven."

Seldom had the great Proconsul been moved so deeply.

"Let us beware, my dear boy, lest the weakening of fiber of the present generation does not undermine our Empire. Pray do not think for one single moment that you will ever regret a union with Adela Rocklaw. As for this other step, I assure you, my dear boy, it is unthinkable."

Having thus unburdened his mind, the Proconsul rose, and, still the prey of deep emotion, swayed majestically forth of the Albany B4.

CHAPTER XVII
IN WHICH WE ARE TAKEN TO VIEW A LITTLE FLAT IN KNIGHTSBRIDGE

MR. PHILIP felt rather limp after the state visit.

"How happy I should be if I were not the son of my father!" was the somewhat unfilial tenor of his thoughts.

Still, he mustered the courage to take Mary out to lunch, but he didn't refer to the recent interview with the Proconsul.

"When is your time up at the Lane, old girl?" inquired the vain young man.

"Quite soon now, Phil-ipp."

"And then what are you doin'?"

"I am going to take Gran'ma to Brighton for a fortnight, and then I'm going to tour the provinces as Lady Agatha in *Kind Hearts and Coronets*, until Mr. Wingrove's new play is put into rehearsal at the Millennium."

Mr. Philip had ordered half a bottle of Number 68, it is rather important to mention, although it had gone up half-a-crown in spite of the fact that some people think it is quite expensive enough already.

"Goin' to be leadin' a full life, ain't you, Polly?"

"Seems like it, doesn't it, Phil-ipp!"

"Well, I think you ought to turn up those beastly provinces, I do really. You are much too good for 'em. I don't know much about it, of course, but it seems to me that such art as yours is wasted on the bally provinces."

"Perhaps you are right, Phil-ipp," said Mary the demure. "But I love the dear old things."

"If I were you, Polly, I should never play out of London, if I had to play at all."

Polly admitted there might be something in this view. Still, she would miss the dear old provinces terribly, and perhaps they might miss her.

And then Number 68 began to display considerable boldness.

"There's a little flat in Knightsbridge, a toppin' little hole, that I think we might go round and look at, old girl, don't you? Very cheap for the position and the landlord will paint it throughout, and we can have possession any time we want it."

Polly didn't mind going to look at it, as she rather liked looking over such things.

The flat was charming. A little high up, perhaps, but there were two delightful rooms that overlooked the park. It was one of the most tempting spots in the metropolis. Yet there was one serious drawback, which in the opinion of Philip, however, was almost a merit. It was likely to be much sought after, said the house-agent; any delay in taking it might be fatal. They could only be allowed a week in which to make up their minds.

Yes, the flat was charming, they agreed, as they walked up Piccadilly. And only a week in which to make up their minds! Still, that was rather providential, if you looked at it from Philip's point of view.

"Wasn't it, Polly?"

"Why do you think so, Phil-ipp?"

"We've got to make up our minds at once, haven't we?"

"I've made up my mind already, Phil-ipp. It is the very place for you; so much moderner and pleasanter and lighter than your chambers."

"Yes, old girl, but I shouldn't think of it for a moment without you."

"Why not, Phil-ipp?"

"Oh, I shouldn't."

A bald reason, perchance, but a manly conviction had given it currency.

"But that's absurd, Phil-ipp. Why should a mere chorus girl—?"

"Look here, Polly," said the fierce young man, "you mustn't suppose I'm going to be chipped by you. If I take that flat, you've got to come and live in it; and, Polly"—and for all they were just opposite the Burlington Arcade, the vain young man took a firm grip of the arm of Mary the obdurate—"I'm bally well goin' to take that flat."

"Are you, Phil-ipp?"

"Yes, and I'm goin' to take it now."

"What!—now, Phil-ipp?"

"At once. Come on back to the house-agents."

"But they are half-a-mile away, Phil-ipp."

"Never mind; it's a nice day for a walk."

"But what about Granny? and what about the great Proconsul; and what about Lady Shelmerdine of Potterhanworth?"

"Oh, let 'em go to blazes—that is, old girl, I beg pardon."

"I should just hope so. And let go my arm, Phil-ipp; people are looking at us."

"Well, let's cut back again."

"But, Phil-ipp."

"You said yourself that it was the nicest position in London, and only nine hundred and fifty a year, which seems rather ridiculous, considerin'—"

"Considering what, Phil-ipp?"

"Considerin' the way they stick you for three rooms and a private bathroom."

"Yes, Phil-ipp, but then think of the address!"

Never, however, in the whole course of his career, not even when he had scored those three goals against Scotland, had Mr. Philip shown more invincible determination than at this moment. If there was not to be a scene in Piccadilly and a paragraph in the evening papers, Mary would have to do as she was told.

"Phil-ipp, you are behaving anyhow."

"Less of it, Polly."

"Less of what, Phil-ipp?"

"Your cheek—you cat."

Unbridled insolence, which we are sure no girl of refined instincts and decent nurture—do you think so, Madam? All the same, that is the manner in which Phil-ipp admonished her, and her salary was a hundred a week, and was likely to be two hundred presently; and the ex-non-commissioned officer on duty at the entrance to the Burlington Arcade pricked up his ears disapprovingly at such language being used to a lady; and his trained observation told him she *was* a lady, although her face had rather more powder on it than it ought to have had; and he wondered whether he would have permitted himself to use such language in such circumstances when he was a young chap in the Guards with one stripe a-courtin' the Missus; and whether the Missus would have had him in spite of his uniform if he had courted her in that way; and whether she wouldn't have been quite right; and whether anybody knew what things were comin' to, because he was quite sure that he didn't. And yes, there the young chap had got hold of her arm again, and, strike his lucky! they were chipping each other like one o'clock; and a dashed pretty girl, and not a bad-looking young chap either. And what were the pair o' turtledoves—as of course a chap of his experience could see with half an eye—quarrelling about? No, not quarrelling exactly, but chipping each other and cross-talking somewhat. And what was it all about? Why, a flat in Knightsbridge. You 'ave it, miss, and be thankful for the chawnce, and think yourself fortunate, which of course you are; and so is he if he gets *you* to go and arrange the flowers in the vases for him.

Down the street again they are going now, though, yet still conducting their heated argument. Granny would be furious, and so would Mother. And Father would cut him out of the succession—which of course he couldn't; and that, perhaps, was almost a pity. She would have to give up the provinces and break her contracts, and everything would be so uncomfortable for everybody—

"Except, old girl, for you and me."

"But that's rather selfish, isn't it, Phil-ipp?"

Phil-ipp dared say it was a little, but yet not altogether, because, after all, it was the way of human nature. Not a very conclusive piece of reasoning, young fellow, but Mistress Polly was bound to admit that, superficial as it was, it would bear thinking upon.

"Be a pal to me, Polly, and I'll be a pal to you, old girl, and we'll be as happy as the birds in the springtime; and you'll see that my people will come round all right, and you'll see that Granny will forgive you!"

And here they were at the office of Messrs. Thompson and Allardyce in Wilton Place—not so far from the Church. And Phil-ipp informed a polite young man, with quite the Oxford manner, that they'd take that flat on a three years' lease from Lady Day—and that, my lords and gentlemen, was how the trick was done. For by the time they had bade adieu to the polite young man with the Oxford manner they were as good as married.

At least, Phil-ipp seemed to think they were. A little previous, perhaps, young fellow; but when you are proceeding full steam ahead at rather more than nine knots an hour, you are rather apt to get a little in front of the time-table, are you not?

"That's the very old thing for us," said Phil-ipp, waving his hand across at the Church. "And I say, old girl, let us see if we can't persuade Granny to give a reception at the Hyde Park Hotel; and I'll persuade old Min Wingrove to bring all the brightest people in London, and we shall rather wipe the eye of No. 88, the corner house, old girl, shan't we, when they see the pictures in the papers?"

"I shall rather like to see you persuading Granny, though, Phil-ipp, particularly after what has occurred."

But Phil-ipp affirmed his manly determination to take the risk, especially as Polly desired to bet a shilling that he daren't.

"Done with you. And I'm hanged if we won't go right away and tackle her."

Whereupon the imperious young man, who was revealing a whole gamut of unexpected qualities, bundled Polly straight into a taxi, demanded to be driven to 10 Bedford Gardens—that magic address—and got in himself.

"I say, old girl," said he, as they sped past the windows of the Button Club, "little Marge can be one of your bridesmaids, can't she?"

"Goose," said Mary.

Yes, and a big one, to be scientifically accurate; yet the proudest and happiest young fellow in all the metropolis just now, possessed by the demon of Damn the Consequences.

CHAPTER XVIII
IN WHICH THE CONSEQUENCES ARE DAMNED WITH NO UNCERTAINTY

MUFFINS and Chayney Tea in Grandmamma's withdrawing-room were not out of place, because the afternoon had been really so strenuous; moreover, Grandmamma herself did not appear to view the guilty pair with the eye of disfavor. But that was breeding, doubtless. Not that Mr. Philip entered into any exhaustive inquiry. When you are in the seventh heaven, even the eye of Edward Bean's goddaughter may be bereft of some of its terrors.

"We had such a lovely lunch at Pagani's, Granny dear."

"Had you, my dear? How interesting!"

Did Granny mean it was interesting, or did she mean it wasn't? You see, you never quite know—do you?—when the elocution of old ladies who have kept pretty good company for about eighty-four summers is so very clear-cut.

"And what do you think, Granny? I have been with Phil-ipp to take a perfectly lovely little flat on a three years' lease in Knightsbridge, overlooking the park."

"With whom have you been, my dear?"

Now we do think that was just a little unkind of Granny, don't you?

Mary's elocution, though, in the opinion of Mr. Hollins—and he's an authority—was worth two hundred a week to the Lane; so it came in very useful just now, and showed that she was not going to be put out of court as easily as all that.

"With Phil-ipp, Granny dear."

"Mr. Shelmerdine, I presume, my dear."

Granny's presumption was correct; and a few more muffins were indicated, Mary seemed to think, for all that her lunch at Pagani's had been so terrific.

All this was merely brushing the ice; it was not really breaking it; and who was going to break it was the problem that now was exercising the manly bosom of Philip. However, they would await that further relay of muffins before they ventured on the pickaxe act.

Muffins with a little salt sprinkled upon 'em do splendidly with Chayney tea, even after a toppin' little lunch at Pagani's. Sometimes, that is. Rather depends, you know, on what quarter the moon is in, and whether Mars and Venus are in conjunction, and Jupiter is in the First House, and the Sun is in Aries, and so on. But given that all these signs and portents are favorable, there is really no reason why muffins and salt and Chayney tea should not be perfectly delectable in Granny's withdrawing-room at twenty minutes past four, even after a champagne luncheon at Pagani's at a quarter to two.

The planetary bodies have been behaving quite nicely this afternoon, so far. Let us hope they will continue to do so.

Jupiter was in the First House, you must please remember; and it was not less than he, as of course the discerning reader has known from the first, who ruled the destinies of this daughter of good fortune who had been endowed with every grace. Therefore it need surprise no one that Mary received a special message by wireless with her second cup of Chayney tea.

"Take Granny into your confidence now, my dear," ran the message. "She has had quite a nice nap; her rheumatism has scarcely troubled her at all to-day; she can't help liking your Phil-ipp, although she has tried her hardest not to; and she is rather inclined to think that it may do no harm to teach—"

Yes, it is doubtless right to keep that part of the message off the records at present.

Mary flung her arms round the neck of Granny, in perilous contiguity to the real-lace-of-Siddons.

"What would you say if Phil-ipp and I were to get married, Granny—quite soon—and we had a sort of a little honeymoon at Brighton with you?"

This was the pickaxe with a vengeance, Miss Mary. Jupiter was very much in the First House this afternoon.

Granny did not say anything immediately. Still, having had a good nap, she sustained the inquiry with admirable composure.

"Very precipitate, my dear, and very unwise, I fear. Have you given sufficient consideration to the Step?"

"We've both thought it over, ma'am," said Mr. Philip, who really felt he was walking on air just now.

"The Step seems singularly unwise to me, Mr. Shelmerdine."

"Why does it, Granny?"

"The reasons, my dear, are many and hardly such as to call for enumeration. In the first place, I understand that Mr. Shelmerdine's family is much opposed to the Match."

"They are bound to come round, ma'am if we give them time," said Mr. Philip.

Grandmamma was not so optimistic.

"Not, of course, Mr. Shelmerdine, if you will permit me to say so, that in the circumstances one regards the sanction of your parents as a *sine quâ non*."

The young man concurred with Grandmamma, more explicitly perhaps than he ought to have done.

"And then there is the question of your vocation, Mr. Shelmerdine. You have none at present, I understand."

"I'm goin' to see about Parliament at once, ma'am."

Grandmamma was bound to admit that the State of Things was not wholly satisfactory to her, but she had had a good nap, and Jupiter was in the First House, and it would really do no harm to Mary to retire from Pantomime and marry a nice young man—which this young man appeared to be, in spite of his mother. Moreover, Grandmamma, being an old lady of spirit, was not altogether averse from teaching some people a lesson. So if she didn't say Yes with any degree of enthusiasm, she didn't say No with any measure of conviction. She belonged to a bygone age which looked at things rather differently from the present one; but if young people wanted very much to marry, old people should not interfere more than was really necessary. All of which goes to show that when Grandmamma had had a good nap and Jupiter was in the First House, she could be as wise and broad-minded as any other old lady.

Still, Grandmamma was afraid that things had altered strangely since her time; but this was a nice young man, in spite of his unfilial attitude; and if a girl really felt she had to marry, there can be nothing so very wrong in marrying a nice young man. But things had altered since her time, thought Granny. Nice young men hardly behaved in this way in 1851, the Exhibition year; which rather goes to show, we are afraid, that the wisest of old ladies are as prone to misread the signs and portents as the lesser mortals.

Mary and Philip, however, kept their exuberance for a crowded and glorious five minutes in the Private Piggery, wherein the lucky young dog inveigled himself for the purpose of putting on the coat with the astrachan collar.

"We must get it all fixed up at once, old girl, and we'll waste no time about it. We'll do it in style, at a church, don't you think? Not of course that I don't prefer the other way, like any other chap if he had his choice, but that's a bit rough on the girl, isn't it?"

Mary thought he was rather a dear to think of the Girl's side; and he thought that she was rather a dear to think that he could be a dear for thinking of his obvious duty. And there they were, you see. Now please don't be cynical, you young ladies of Newnham and Girton; it will be your turn presently, and when it comes, my dears, take the advice of your Uncle John, and behave as much as you can like Philip and Mary. But see that the door of the Private Piggery is closed when Jane is passing, otherwise it may have a tendency to put ideas in the heads of pretty young parlor-maids, and Grandmamma has found occasion to tell Miss Jane privately more than once that she has quite sufficient of Those already.

"We'll send out invitations for anywhere you like, old girl, and we'll get old Minnie Wingrove to collect all the brightest people in London; and the papers will make such a fuss that we shan't half wipe the eye of Grosvenor Square, shall we?"

"Naughty Phil-ipp. You mustn't never wipe the eye of no one."

Still, she had rather forgotten, hadn't she, young ladies of Newnham and Girton, that Mr. Philip was not yet an archangel in a large way of trade, although apparently that was her ambition for him. But you won't think any the worse of her, will you? It's all in the game, my dears, and a very nice game, too, if you play it slowly.

How long would it take her to get her trousseau?

No, you young bachelors of Cam and Isis, that was not a clever question. But one must expect this sort of thing of an amateur now and then. Philip, young friend, your inquiry should have been differently expressed.

And what was Mary's answer to the foolish question? Why, just what yours would have been, young ladies.

Mary didn't know how long it would take her to get her trousseau.

We agree with you, my dears, that only a perfect Silly would have been guilty of any such inquiry.

Should they go to Algiers for the honeymoon?

"Yes, Phil-ipp, but who is going to look after Granny at Brighton? She goes there every March, you know, by advice."

"We'll go to Brighton, then," said Philip, "or a tour round the world, or anywhere."

So they left it at that; and the lucky young dog proceeded on foot to the nearest of his clubs, for all that he felt like an airship really; and engaged in a game of snooker pool with two eminent criminal barristers—that is to say, two eminent members of the Common Law Bar—and was very soon the poorer by the sum of two pounds sterling.

Then the young man sat down and wrote a little line to Mary, which ran to four pages, and was absolutely superfluous, because it was really about nothing at all except to remind her that she was the dearest and best, etc. Fortunately he had the good sense to tear it up, so that not one was a penny the worse for an ill-written, and miss-spelt, and hopelessly ungrammatical effusion, and that notwithstanding that the writer had enjoyed all the advantages of a regular classical education. And then Mr. Wingrove sauntered into the Club in his magnificent mannah, and then the floodgates opened.

"I've done it, Min."

The great man was almost afraid the too-familiar groundling would cast himself upon his neck.

"Done what, and why have you done it?" was the unsympathetic inquiry of one whose heart was really as ripe as his judgment.

A long and impassioned recital, of course; and Minnie must help to make it a really great occasion, in order to wipe the eye of No. 88, the corner house.

Mr. Wingrove evinced no particular enthusiasm for this operation, and that was as it should have been, because the attitude of Mr. Philip was fearfully unfilial. Do not for a moment let us pretend it wasn't. But what was a chap to do?

In the circumstances, perhaps, thought Arminius Wingrove, it would show good feeling to be married by the Registrar.

"I'm hanged if we'll be," said Philip, "unless she really wants it; and of course no girl does."

"Then it appears to me," said Arminius Wingrove, "that you should go to church as quietly as possible in the absence of your parents."

"That's their look-out, though," said this dogged Briton. "They'll get an invitation; and if they like to come, so much the better; and if they don't, why it's up to us to show that we can do without 'em."

But Arminius Wingrove was quite a man of the world, you know. If your admirable parents consent to grace this celebration, said that great man, I will exert any little influence I may possess to raise large type in the Leading Morning Journal. But if your admirable parents decide not to grace this celebration, let only the chosen few be present, because to my mind good taste requires it.

These were wise words of Arminius Wingrove. Pray ponder 'em, you young bachelors of Cam and Isis. And you young ladies of Newnham and Girton, should you ever—which we hope you'll never—go to church in a mechanically propelled vehicle without the consent of your parents, please to remember that in the mature judgment of the *arbiter elegantiarum*, good taste requires that you shall be married in your traveling dress, and that you shall go in by the side entrance.

CHAPTER XIX
A GREAT OCCASION

MOTHER was the first to see in the *Morning Post* that a marriage had been arranged, and would shortly take place. She handed the excellent journal across the table to Father with a sphinxlike countenance. But, as Mr. Jennings subsequently informed the housekeeper, Mrs. Meeson, in a private colloquy in the pantry, his lordship took the blow with resignation.

"No more than I've been expecting for some little time past, Agatha," said the great Proconsul.

But the wife of his bosom was dumb with dismay.

"Agatha," said the Proconsul, after Mr. Jennings had quitted the scene, "have you seen the Person?"

"I have, Wally; and I am strongly of opinion that Philip is out of his mind."

Not very comforting, was it?

There was only one thing to be done, though, and that was what generations of excellent parents have had to do before them—namely, and to wit, To Grin and Bear It.

Frankly, the Governing Classes were not specially good at grinning, but they bore the blow with resignation tempered by quiet dignity. They had done nothing to deserve the unmerited Cross of Fortune—the Reverend Canon Fearon came in person to inform them of that. Their lives were virtuous; their aspirations blameless; their good works manifest. But the ways of Providence were inscrutable—cream, please, but no sugar, thank you—why the blow should have fallen upon them of all people—a little brown bread and butter—was one more familiar instance of the things that passed all understanding.

Consolation for the spirit, you see, was at the service of Mother. Father received that form of sustenance also—at the Helicon, that temple of light.

"My dear Shelmerdine," said Ch: Bungay, the friend of his youth, "it is good to know that the blow is sustained with the accustomed resignation of a true Christian."

It was by no means clear, however, that in Mount Street the Christian Ticket was sweeping the polls at this period. The resignation of Pa, in the opinion of rumor, was a little less pronounced than that of his neighbors.

The butler gave notice the same afternoon. On the following morning her ladyship's maid declined to stay to have her head bitten off, and went to the length of saying so. Even the Reverend Canon Fearon was constrained to think that an Irish peerage was hardly the same as the home-made article.

It was an unlucky state of things, said the friends of both families. Rather depended upon how you looked at it though, thought the People Next Door. A Love Match is sometimes superior to a *Mariage de Convenance*, thought Ann Veronica, who had just returned from Dresden. Perhaps She Won't Be Quite So Stuck Up Now, wrote the Flapper from Eastbourne. He's swopped her for the absolute nicest gal in London, anyhow, said the Probationer in His Majesty's Horseguards. And Mamma said that she was surprised that Percy should talk in that way; and his Papa hoped that *he* wouldn't go making a fool of himself; and the Reverend Canon Fearon, when he called to ask the People Next Door what they thought about it, was rather inclined to agree with all parties, since yesterday at luncheon his Bishop had given utterance to the profoundly searching moral observation that the streams of tendency were apt to overlook their banks a little by the time the rising generation was ready to embark.

It is good to know that the Great did not lack spiritual aid in their hour of tribulation. But Pa in Mount Street and the Seventh Unmarried Daughter were not so chastened as they might have been, perhaps; and Father and Mother still went out to dinner regularly, in spite of this humiliation.

Nevertheless, Father and Mother declined the invitation to St. James's, Wilton Place, and to the reception afterwards, which, if they would consent to grace it, would be held by Grandmamma, her eighty-four years notwithstanding, at the Hyde Park Hotel.

The reply of Mother was a model of dignity, but the reception was not held. It could have been, certainly, since there were a number of people who would have been delighted to come; but the goddaughter of Bean, in her conscious strength, agreed with Arminius Wingrove that it would show good feeling not to wipe the eye of Grosvenor Square.

The nuptials of Philip and Mary were not so brilliant as they might have been, perhaps, had Father and Mother attended them, but everything was very nice and cheerful all the same. The bridesmaids were five ladies of the Profession, including Marge; and excluding Timothy, who was a page in an extraordinarily smart blue suiting, which he had to be most careful how he sat in it. It wasn't Dr. Bridge who played the organ, but a gentleman quite as clever, think some who heard him on the festal afternoon. The ex-brother-officer remembered where the ring was put; Philip remembered to kiss Mary—and, you young bachelors of Cam and Isis you will hurt Her feelings awfully if you should forget that part of the ceremony, so kindly make a note of the foregoing—and everybody thought the Bride looked absolutely sweet, and that Philip was a very fortunate young man.

And in the judgment of Herb and Arminius Wingrove, Grandmamma, in a fine new hat, was right in the foreground of the picture.

Everything was just as it should have been; everybody looked pleased and happy; and when forth the organ pealed the noble work by Mendelssohn all agreed that they made a mighty handsome pair.

There was no reception at the Hyde Park Hotel; but Mr. Hollins bade all and sundry attend a tea-party on the classic boards of Drury. Grandmamma cut the cake that Mr. Hollins had provided; and Marge and Timothy ate thereof—not a crumb more than was good for 'em, although both came very near the limit. And then Mr. Hollins made a speech which we feel obliged to quote verbatim in this place.

Said Mr. Hollins: "Ladies and Gentlemen, I sincerely hope this is not the end of a great career. (Hear, hear.) I have my doubts about it, though. I have seen this sort of thing before. (Cheers and laughter.) We all envy the Bridegroom, and I am afraid we shall find it hard to forgive him, if, as our prophetic souls have feared, he robs a great profession of a chief ornament. (Hear, hear.) But if this is a grudge we may have to cherish against him, there is a service he has rendered to us that must always redound to his credit. He is the means of summoning back to these classic boards, after an absence, she tells me, of forty-three years, one of the great figures of a bygone generation, whose name was as familiar as a household word throughout the length and breadth of the land, before even the improvident parents of the majority of those of us who are present this afternoon had arranged about our cradles. Ladies and Gentlemen, I refer to that true ornament of her profession, Mrs. Cathcart. (Loud and prolonged applause.) We are exceedingly proud to have her among us; and some of you will doubtless boast to your grandchildren that you have had the opportunity of drinking the health of this famous and venerable lady, because, after Sir Herbert has proposed the health of the Bride, it is to be my great privilege to propose that of one of the truest ornaments the English stage has known." (Great enthusiasm.)

This was not all by any means that Mr. Hollins was moved to say on this historic occasion. But you will be able to gather, doubtless, from the general tenor of the famous Manager's remarks, that the Bride was quite within her rights in being moved to tears, and that the Bridegroom had warrant for the otherwise irrelevant observation, "I wish the Mater had been here, old girl, that's all."

And then in grim earnest the bowl began to flow; enthusiasm began to wax parlous; and the wretched Bridegroom had to get up on his hind legs, feeling quite as uncertain about the knee-joints as this unfortunate quadruped of ours, and proceeded to apologize very sweetly and humbly to the profession for having robbed it of one of whom it had a right to be proud, and who was a thousand and one times too good, at a conservative estimate, for the chap who had brought her back from St. James's, Wilton Place. And candor forces us to admit that this idle, rich young fellow, who had made a good many enemies by his act of presumption, didn't materially add to their number by the speech which he made, which, if not exactly that of an orator, was yet manly and sincere and unaffected and no discredit to the famous Twin Brethren who had nurtured his youth.

CHAPTER XX
LOVE'S YOUNG DREAM

THE first fortnight of the honeymoon was spent in Paris. They looked at pictures and saw new plays, and went racing on Sunday, and walked in the gardens of Versailles, and did a hundred other cheerful things, and were most marvelously happy. And Mary, who hardly cared a bit about such matters, bought herself a new hat.

They were tempted to go on to the Riviera, but duty prevailed and they went to Brighton on the fourteenth day. Grandmamma had gone to that famous physician on her twenty-sixth annual excursion; and Mary felt she must keep her eye upon her, for all that she was such a hale and vigorous old thing.

Grandmamma was discovered in very nice lodgings along the sea-front, in the care of a landlady, very civil and voluble, and a mistress of the art of plain cooking. Everything very pleasant and comfortable, and a sitting-room with a balcony overlooking the King's Parade. It really seemed that the young couple might put in a fortnight very profitably here, while their chosen residence in the metropolis was being painted throughout.

They had their little adventures, of course, this happy pair, because Brighthelmstone is the home of so many romances. For one thing, they attracted attention when they walked abroad. Philip was sure that it was the hat from Paris; Mary was absolutely convinced that it was the coat with the astrachan collar and the spats by Grant and Cockburn. But what really impressed the floating population of Brighthelmstone was the comeliness of both; the simple pleasure they derived from the society of each other; their abounding joy in being allowed to walk about this underrated planet.

Had this natural history of nothing in particular the least pretensions to cynicism, which the world looks for in a modern romance, the happy pair would be disillusioned already. They should have been profoundly weary of one another by the fourth day in Paris, according to all the rules of the game. He should have discovered that she was shallow and half-educated, and consequently a bit of a bore when she brought the same face downstairs three mornings consecutively for *café au lait*. She should have discovered that he was selfish and vain, and that in his heart he didn't think that Her belongings were equal to His, and that he saw already what a fool he had made of himself. And that being the case, she should have grown conscious of her own inferiority, and begun to hate him because she had done so, and wish herself back again on the boards.

Moreover, had the Author really known his business, they should have quarrelled bitterly on the subject of Grandmamma. Who has heard of a newly-married pair giving up the Riviera and going to Brighton to look after an old lady of eighty-four with all her faculties? He should have been obdurate, and she should have shed tears of bitterness. He should have secretly cursed his gods for the blindness that had shackled him for the rest of his days; she should have had thoughts of the Seine, and have given them expression. He should have yielded when he should have stood firm; she should have despised him for his weakness. They should have snarled at one another all the way to Brighton, and Grandmamma should have been very disagreeable when they got there, and not in the least need of their presence. But candor forces us to make full confession of our incompetence. Because none of these things came to pass.

Very much the contrary, let us assure you. Their good looks and their air of general happiness were the envy of all people of observation along the sea-front. Still they had their adventures, and some at least will have to be recorded.

One morning, as they proceeded almost arm-in-arm, but not quite, looking as though they had just bought the cosmos at five per cent. discount for cash, and were completely satisfied with the transaction, they walked right into a bath chair which was accompanied by a Sealskin Coat and a Himalayan Dust Spaniel.

Salutations necessary, being right up against each other, so to speak.

"How d'ye do, Adela," said the Culprit, who in his happiness seemed to have nothing to conceal and nothing to defend. "You know my wife, don't you?"

The wind was certainly blowing very chilly from the northern heights this morning. 'Tis a little way it has in March at Brighthelmstone.

Pa was not so bad as he might have been.

"Introdooce me," said His Britannic Majesty's former Ambassador to Persia.

So Pa was introduced to the Bride; and she afterwards told Hubby that he was like any other Pa, only a little more so. And, she being a girl of sense as well as of spirit, Pa didn't seem to mind talking to her a little, particularly as she knew so much about rheumatism, because it was Granny's complaint.

Had Lord Warlock tried the new treatment?

No; what was that?

The new treatment called for explanation. Duly forthcoming with minuteness and lucidity. No; not a designing minx, mesdames, altogether. Tact, certainly; but it had its roots, remember, in a heart as sound as a bell, overflowing with practical sympathy for all the world and his wife.

"Grandmamma has a book about it, and a special apparatus. It has done her a power of good—a power of good. She will be delighted to lend them, I'm sure—that's if you care, Lord Warlock. It's a wonderful invention, and I'll bring it round this afternoon, and show you how it works."

"Thank yah," said the Ex-Ambassador to Persia. "And I'll be devilish obliged."

Hubby, though, was not doing quite so well with the Sealskin Coat. Brighthelmstone so dull and tiresome, so cold, and hotels so unpleasant; and all the time the fair speaker announced these drawbacks she looked not so much at the young man who ought to have married her, but out of the corner of a cold blue eye at the person who was talking to Pa as though she knew all about his complaint.

"Thank yah," said Pa, touching his hat, one of those hard, square felt ones whose ugliness nought can surpass, as the procession passed on. "The Suffolk. Don't forget."

A designing minx—madam, we do not agree. Mere tact, you know. And it was perfectly clear that her quick, spontaneous, practical sympathy had left its mark even on that unpromising subject.

Not such a fool as I thought he was not to have taken this gal off my hands, reflected the Uncompromising Subject within the precincts of his bath chair. And then, with the air of one who nurses an injury, he proceeded to inquire of the Seventh Unmarried Daughter—

"Well, Addie my gal, what do you think of the Mésalliance?"

"One doesn't profess to be a judge of chorus girls," said the rude girl, jerking the unfortunate Himalayan Dust Spaniel right off his feet.

Actually rude to her Pa, you see. Really, miss! But are you quite doing her Justice, young friend? says Mr. G-ls-w-thy. Do you think the girl has had fair play? because, frankly, I don't. Born with a silver spoon in her mouth; every whim gratified; never had a soul to cross or deny her; always able to go to the Stores and order what she wanted within reason; never rubbed her shoulders against life in its sterner aspects like your more fortunate heroine; never changed an iota since she used to bully her nurse. Fact is, young friend, says Mr. G-lsw-thy, you can't expect people who have had a plumb wicket to bat on all their born days to play as well as those who have been well schooled on more difficult pitches. Mind, I don't say that Adela would ever have been as nice as your Mary, but I feel very strongly that under fairer conditions there is a great deal of good in the girl that must have reached the surface.

Her manner would always have been a bit against her, of course, Pa not being over-rich for his position; the eye would always have been a little contemptuous, since it was its nature to; but there were certain things in the girl that a hard, uphill, unprotected life in the great textile towns of England, Scotland, Ireland and Wales, a trip to Australia and South Africa, and a six months' tour in the United States and Canada might have developed considerably. But, concludes the Sage, it would have remained a nice question whether she would have been as well fitted to be a Mayfair hostess, or to arrange a shooting party, or to ride in Leicestershire, or to attend the gracious Consort of our Sovereign, as she is at present.

These alternatives are of a character that we are not competent to express an opinion upon; but, at present, Mr. Philip seemed to be in no doubt as to the wisdom of his choice; and really that seems rather important, particularly as the young fellow overflowed with happiness as he walked along the King's Parade, longing to take the arm of the nicest girl in Brighthelmstone into his keeping, and yet fearing to do so since it was rather advertising the fact that they had only been married a fortnight.

"I say, kidlet"—overpass the epithet, you Old Married People; you know you have once been as guilty yourselves—"you talked like a book to the Belted One, didn't you, what?"

"Yes, Phil-ipp, the poor old dear. The same complaint as Granny. I'm going to take him her apparatus and show him how to work it, and I've guaranteed that he will be able to walk upstairs after he has used it a week."

"Have you, though? But how you dared, I'm blest if I know."

"Cow-yard, Phil-ipp. He's rather a dear, really."

"A most disagreeable old gentleman, and the worst manners of any Privy Councillor in London."

"A libel, Phil-ipp. I'm sure he's not so bad as all that. Anyhow, if he is, I shall try and reform him."

CHAPTER XXI
ADVENTURES RARE AND STRANGE

IT was opposite the Magnificent that they came upon adventure the second. Two gentlemen of somewhat informal aspect, one of whom was in need of a shave, and both of whose hats were light green, greeted Mary as if they were half afraid to do so, and yet didn't like to pass her by.

"Thought perhaps you mightn't remember us, Mary."

"Remember *you*, Horace! Could I ever forget you? And why, I declare it's Johnny?"

And Mary shook hands with Horace and Johnny so simply and so cordially—for all that she had married a Toff—that they were obliged to confess that they were quite sure she couldn't.

The next moment Horace and Johnny were being introduced to the Toff; with rather a display of wariness on their part, because provincial stars who have had to carve out their own destiny have not much use for the Breed, and they owed him a grudge as well for having robbed the profession of an idol. So when the Toff held out his hand and appeared pleased to meet them, it was not so certain that they were pleased to meet him.

"Horace Allwright, Philip, the very first Pickles I ever played to—and the best."

"Oh, go hon, John Willie," said the Star of the North, blushing to the roots of his hair, which was red and, therefore, made his pleasure the more conspicuous. But he wasn't going to stand any swank from Eton and Ch: Ch:; and the rather fierce eye of this fine natural comedian said so pretty distinctly.

Mary was undefeated, though, and Johnny Dubosque not being so great a man as Horace Allwright, and consequently having less in the way of dignity to look after, was soon behaving as if nothing had happened.

"But I expect you'll never come to the provinces again, Polly," said Johnny Dubosque sadly. "I said to Horace it was all up with *us* as soon as you got to the Lane. But you'll be turning up the perfession altogether now."

Mary said it might be so, and Johnny Dubosque sighed deeply, and informed the Toff in a burst of confidence that her place could never be filled. And the Toff—for all that the Twin Brethren were not a little discomposed by hearing one who was not a fellow alumnus speak of the wife as Polly—apologized so nicely to the Perfession for having done what it had done, that Johnny Dubosque, who had a generous heart, felt not a little inclined to forgive him, and Horace Allwright somewhat waived the question of his dignity.

"Come across to the Magnificent, old chap, and 'ave a drink," said Horace Allwright in a sudden and overwhelming burst of hospitality.

The Toff accepted the invitation, and for that act of grace, my lords and gentlemen, honor is due to the Twin Brethren, who as *you* do not require to be told, would have disbursed current coin of the realm to shirk this obvious duty. But it would never do to make an enemy of a friend of Mary's. Therefore the Twin Brethren allowed themselves to be led across the road about as cheerfully as a lamb is led to the slaughter; and the grandees of the place stared very hard at the entrance of These Theatrical People; and the Twin Brethren devoutly hoped that no stray member of the Button Club was lying concealed among the ferns.

Modest libations were ordered by Mr. Horace Allwright in a rather loud manner, with a lemon squash for Mary, although this was mere natural politeness on her part.

"We shall not see her equal as Cinderella, not in our time, my lord," said Mr. Horace Allwright in a very audible aside to the Toff, in order to keep in touch with the public.

"Of course you will, Horace, and many a better one," said the Uncrowned Queen of Blackhampton, having with her ready tact and her quick observation detected the plight of the unhappy Twin Brethren who were blenching a little under their tan.

Not so far off were a pair of Contemporaries, out of sight, perchance, yet by no means out of hearing.

"Why, if it isn't that damned fool Shel, with his mésalliance!"

"No—yes—my God!"

"Rather nice, though, in spite of the friends of the family."

"Let us go and pull the leg of the silly old fool, and make him turn out for us to-morrow."

Whereupon the Contemporaries rose from their table, very finely grown young men and superbly tailored, as all distinguished athletes should be.

"Why, Shel, old man, how are you?"

Hearty hand-grips were exchanged, although the Twin Brethren were not feeling so very robust at present.

"Fancy meeting you here!"

There was no particular reason why they shouldn't meet there, but it is always a useful opening card. And then the Olympians were introduced to Mary, and pretty keenly did they scrutinize her, although they pretended so well that they were doing nothing of the sort that it would have taken a woman to have told what the sly dogs were at.

And then Miss Mary trod very hard on the foot of Eton and Ch: Ch:, which begged pardon humbly and introduced Mr. Horace Allwright and Mr. Johnny Dubosque, and piously hoped to its Maker that it hadn't got mixed in their names.

"Pleased to meet you, gentlemen," said Mr. Horace Allwright spaciously. "'Ave a drink."

The Olympians had had a drink already, but they had no objection to having another; and this accommodating disposition caused Mary to take them into favor at once, and they were invited to sit down.

"'Ere's a health to the bride," said Mr. Johnny Dubosque.

"Thank you, Johnny."

"I was just a-tellin' his lordship," said Mr. Horace Allwright, "that she was absolutely the finest Cinderella I've ever played to, and I've played to some of the first in my time, let me tell you. Good 'ealth, gentlemen."

And while Mr. Horace Allwright was happily engaged in pledging the health of the company, Mary proceeded to transfix the first Olympian with such a staunch, straight and demure gray eye that the heart of the famous athlete was literally pinned against the antimacassar of yellow plush upholstery which had been provided by the hotel for the use of its patrons.

"His lordship's drawn a winner in the lottery, gentlemen," continued Mr. Horace Allwright, and in this the first Olympian was strongly inclined to concur.

"Cut it out, Horace," said the Uncrowned Queen of Blackhampton with a very arch glance at Johnny Dubosque. "It isn't cricket, is it, Johnny? in these fashionable watering-places. And I won't have you pull the leg of my Phil-ipp by calling him my lord, when he's promised me solemn to stand for Mr. Lloyd George."

"You haven't, Shel?" quoth the Olympians, feeling it was up to them to say something, and that this was something they might say.

"Oh, but he has," said the Uncrowned Queen, "and I should never have married him if he hadn't—should I, Phil-ipp?"

And she transfixed both the Olympians this time with that demure glance of tremendous impact.

"Oh, but I say, Mrs. Shel," quoth the first Olympian, beginning to feel a glow within, "what about his Governor, you know?"

"I don't know about his Governor, Mr. Wilbraham, because I'm not received in the Family at present."

And this time the glance came right home to the Twin Brethren, who at once began to feel like bucking up a little.

"But you are bound to be, Mrs. Shel, aren't you?" said Mr. Wilbraham with great Tact.

"Why am I bound to be?" inquired the Uncrowned Queen, whose good gray eye had begun to play the dickens with the second Olympian.

"Oh, you are, you know. Isn't she, Toddles?"

Toddles was strongly of opinion that she was.

"Well, of course, if you both really think that—"

But in the secret recesses of his nature, Toddles was even more strongly of opinion that if she persisted in looking at him in that way he would be bound to kiss her.

"Are you and Mr. Wilbraham any good at snooker? Yes, I can see it in your eyes. Well, Phil-ipp and Johnny and I will play the three of you for a sovereign."

"Done with you, Mrs. Shel," said the Olympians with promptitude.

And then Mrs. Shelmerdine looked very demurely at Horace Allwright, and imposed the condition that the stakes should be deposited with the marker, as her success in life was entirely due to the fact that she never trusted on principle a man who came from Leeds.

"But I come from Leeds myself," said Toddles, who, of course, was none other than the popular Yorkshire cricketer when he had time to spare for the game.

"Why not?"

"Yes; why not? But how could you tell I came from Leeds, Mrs. Shelmerdine?"

"By your trousers."

Horace and Johnny roared long and loud at this brilliant sally. The natural insight of those famous comedians had taught them already that if Toddles had a weakness, it was an undue pride in his trousers, which of course the young man was quite entitled to have, since they were the work of Mr. F-ster of London and Oxford.

"Now, don't let her pull your leg, old man," said Philip, who, as usual a little behind in the uptake, had only just begun his roar. "She'll rag the life out of you if you'll let her."

Without further preface or apology, an adjournment was made to the billiard saloon, which was down a very long corridor. *En route*, Mr. Wilbraham, whose name in athletic circles was Weary William, because he was never in a hurry, confided to Toddles that she was every bit as nice off the stage as she was on it.

To which Toddles, in whose cognomen a meaning has yet to be discovered, rejoined that "He was always a far-seein' old swine."

Mary liked a light cue, and used it in a manner which did not suggest the novice. By what means she had gained her skill, it would be best, perhaps, not to inquire. At least, it is hardly likely that Grandma had taught her.

The Olympians also had misspent their youth a little, and Horace Allwright's father had been a billiard-marker, so it was quite as well, perhaps, that Mary was so skillful, and that Philip was able to say he was a pupil of Mr. John Roberts, Junior. The master might not have been very proud of him, though, to judge by the way he started; but he improved as the game went on, and as Johnny Dubosque knew Stevenson to talk to, the game was quite worth looking at in the opinion of a somewhat saturnine-looking gentleman who sat in the corner drinking Schweppe's ginger ale, and picking winners out of the *Sportsman*.

The game was twenty-nine all, and there was only one ball left on the table, and that was "a sitter" on the brink of the left-hand top pocket, which Mary, who had played amazingly well all through, had left there to her unfeigned sorrow. It was all over, bar the shouting, when Toddles proceeded to deliver his cue, for it really was a shot that one who had used his youth as he had done ought not to have missed with his eyes shut.

In the most unaccountable manner the famous center forward missed the shot with his eyes wide open, promptly apostrophized his Maker, and insisted in paying the stakes.

"You did that a-purpose, Mr. Toddles," said Mary sternly, "and I scorn to take your money. I am not a suffragist yet, but that's the kind of thing to make me one. Why, a woman can't even have fair play at a game like snooker."

Followed a heated controversy. Mr. Toddles would not confess to his guilt, which was really so flagrant that Mary wondered how he dared deny the charge. Horace Allwright and Weary William lied circumstantially to support the misdemeanant, but Mary refused to accept the stakes, and in this we venture to think she was right.

No, Toddles, young friend, it is not the way to produce a race of sportswomen. Your intentions were of the highest, certainly, but your charming opponent had taken such degrees in the school of experience, although she was hardly twenty-four at present, that she didn't even think it polite.

There was only one method of composing the quarrel, and that was to play the match over again. And this time, it is sad to relate of three excellent sportsmen, good care was taken that there should be no doubt whatever about the issue.

"And now you have taken us on at this game, Shel," said the first Olympian, "we shall expect you to turn out for us to-morrow against Brighton and Hove Albion."

"But I haven't kicked a ball for years."

"So much the worse for you. The match is for the benefit of the widow and young children of a good chap, and you were always a great draw for the public."

"Was I?" said Mr. Philip apprehensively, for he read in the eyes of Mary that his doom was sealed.

"Were you, Phil-*ipp*! Might never have kicked three goals against Scotland, mightn't you? Why, of course you'll play; especially as it's a benefit match."

"But I haven't kicked a ball for years and years, and I've got no gear either."

"We'll soon fix you up with some gear, won't we, Mrs. Shel?" said the exultant Olympians.

"Ra-*ther*."

Poor Philip protested bitterly; but he knew, alas! that he would have to bow to the inevitable. At a quarter-past three on the morrow, after an absence of four years, he was doomed to reappear in the ranks of the famous amateur team whom he had helped to make history.

CHAPTER XXII
IN WHICH PHILIP RENEWS HIS YOUTH

WHEN Horace and Johnny resumed their walk along the King's Parade, they felt at least two inches taller for having rubbed shoulders with the aristocracy. Everybody does, Sir, says Mr. Thackeray; and no one is a penny the worse for this national feeling, we venture to hope, provided it is not carried to excess. Certainly the girls of Brighthelmstone had a rare treat for the rest of the day, Johnny and Horace putting on wonderful "side," and setting their hats at an angle warranted to kill at sight.

The Idol of the Profession ought never to have married a Toff. Still, they all did it if they had the chance, so you could hardly blame her. But the great thing was, she hadn't changed at all. She was just the same honest pal as when she played at the Queen's at Leeds. Her heart was still in the right place in spite of her elevation. It wasn't always so, but it was in this case. She was one of the very best, and she had proved it that morning to five places of decimals recurring, by not being ashamed of old friends.

Thus you see, my lords and gentlemen, in spite of the fact that Horace and Johnny swaggered along the King's Parade in a way that Eton and Oxford never do—do they?—and that *you* would hardly have cared to accept their invitation to cross the road and 'ave a drink at the good old Magnificent—at least, not when the wife was with you—they were really modest men at heart, as most men are if they ever attain to reasonable eminence in their particular walk of life.

"Fancy *you* marrying a Toff!" Horace Allwright had whispered to Mary over his beer.

"Why shouldn't one, pray?" was the rejoinder of the future Lady Shelmerdine of Potterhanworth.

"You are right—why not?" said Horace. "Because, after all, you are a Toff yourself."

And in the middle of the King's Parade the famous comedian reaffirmed the conviction.

"And he's not a bad chap either, considerin'," said Horace. "Damn good snooker, anyhow, and the best inside right that ever kicked a ball, except Steve Bloomer, and we'll go and see him play to-morrow."

"What do *you* think?" said Johnny Dubosque expansively, laying siege to a nursemaid—and a pretty one, too, in a very smart bonnet.

This is all quite trivial and doesn't really help the narrative, but the point we wish to make is, that our friend Philip had not exactly wasted his morning, whatever may be the views of parents and guardians upon the subject. This idle, rich young man, instead of alienating sympathy for his class, had added two recruits to the chosen band of its friends and admirers. He had behaved very well in difficult circumstances, and he had now two more friends spread over the world than he had started out with in life. Consequently he had increased the public stock of human amenity, and we venture, therefore, to think that his morning had been very far from wasted.

Mary also had done very well, having brought Mr. Philip out of his shell a bit. Quite an eventful morning; nothing to what the following afternoon would be, though, when he had to play *v* Brighton and Hove Albion for the benefit of the widow and young family of the late Joe McPherson. After the match at snooker, Philip was borne off in triumph to Brighthelmstone's leading sports emporium to find a white flannel shirt about his size and a pair of dark-blue knickerbockers, and a very smart pair of stockings, and some shin-guards, and, most important of all, a pair of boots that would fit him.

The morrow would be a great ordeal, particularly in a bran-new pair of boots, for a chap who had not kicked a ball for four years, but Mary was adamant, and the Olympians, too. A benefit match; a great draw for the public; do him all the good in the world.

"And we'll have some special bills printed," said Toddles with something suspiciously like a wink at the future Lady Shelmerdine of Potterhanworth.

"Oh, no, for God's sake!"

"You shouldn't have given it away, Mr. Toddles," expostulated Mary.

"You won't half get a licking to-morrow," said the shop boy with broad satisfaction as he tied up the parcel. "The Albion's playing its full league team."

"But the Olympians are playing the team that won the Arthur Dunn Cup," said the future Lady Shelmerdine of Potterhanworth, with something suspiciously like a wink at Toddles, "and if you've any sense, boy—and you ought to have lots with that high forehead—you won't put your weekly sixpence on the Albion to-morrow."

Great things were promised for the morrow, but Mary put in some more useful work that afternoon. About four o'clock she carried round Granny's apparatus, together with the book of the words, to Pa at the

Suffolk. She was received by His Britannic Majesty's Ex-Ambassador to Persia; had the honor of drinking tea with him; discussed rheumatism in general; showed the working of the apparatus, and even demonstrated it, not without symptoms of success; and in less than half an hour had made such an incursion upon the regard of this widower of ripe experience, that he was fain to inform the seventh unmarried daughter over dinner, "that young Shelmerdine's wife was a devilish sensible woman, and he hoped to see more of her."

Tact; natural goodness of heart; a sunny temper, and a practical disposition; these be great qualities, you young ladies of Newnham and Girton. The widower of ripe experience was a mighty shrewd judge of your kind, although a severe one, because he had not chosen so wisely as he might have done in the First Instance; and in the Second Instance, had he chosen less wisely he might have been more comfortable; but he knew a good, sensible, sound-hearted young woman when he saw one, and he knew quite enough of her importance to the world not to undervalue her. Hence the "chorus girl" had already made a considerable incursion—and the pearl necklace and the simple black dinner-frock which had cost a hundred guineas, and the hair *très bien coiffés* were a little cooler to Pa than usual, and nibbled more salted almonds than was good for 'em.

The apparatus could do Pa no harm; Mr. Joseph O'Flaherty, his lordship's valet, was strongly of that opinion, and said so to her ladyship's maid, whose name was Adèle, but had been changed to Lisette for obvious reasons. Whether the apparatus actually brought material benefit to Pa, we are not in a position to state positively; but there can be no doubt that, indirectly, the apparatus had a tonic effect upon Pa's general system.

The day of the match had now arrived, and that was such an important affair, being for the benefit of the widow and five young children of the late Joe McPherson, as honest a player as ever handled the ball when the referee wasn't looking, that it will be necessary to supply some sort of an account of this historic function.

It was a crowded and glorious day for Mary and Philip; and it really started pretty soon after breakfast, when those famous men, namely and to wit, Toddles and W. W., rang the bell of Granny's lodgings and were ushered into the front sitting-room on the first floor. At the moment of their arrival Mary was trying over on the piano, which had several of its notes intact, although none of them in tune, the latest manifestation of the genius of Mr. Rubens.

"Please, don't let us interrupt you," said W. W., laying a suspicious-looking brown paper parcel on the table.

Mary, however, took this for mere natural politeness.

"Oh, you've brought them, I see. *Do* let me look."

Now what was it, do you suppose, that she wanted to look at? Wait, if you please, until W. W. has cut the string of the parcel with a pocketknife that was given him by his Aunt Marian, contrary to the advice of his parents, about the time he wore his H. M. S. *Indomitable.*

Five hundred handbills were in the parcel, printed by the Brighthelmstone Steam Printing Company, Ltd. Mary seized eagerly the one that was solemnly presented to her by W. W., while Toddles, more demonstrative than he, grinned effusively from ear to ear.

Mary read the following:

GRAND FOOTBALL MATCH FOR THE BENEFIT
OF THE WIDOW AND FIVE CHILDREN
OF THE LATE JOE McPHERSON.

The Olympians *v* Brighton and Hove Albion.

The Honorable Philip Shelmerdine has arrived in
Brighton, and will positively reappear at inside
right this afternoon at 3:15.

"I think that will about fix it, Mrs. Shel," said W. W. proudly. "We'll have these distributed all over the place; and we've got some bigger ones, too, to go on the hoardings."

But Philip, who at that moment was taking his fox terrier for a short constitutional, had seen the hoardings already. Thus, when he came in about five minutes later, bloodshed nearly ensued. A feeble jest, undoubtedly, but one of the penalties of athletic greatness. And when Mary insisted upon distributing with her own gloved hands these handbills to every passer-by along the King's Parade, they came within hail of their first quarrel. To be sure, the majority of the recipients thought they were Votes for Women, and didn't look at them, and those who did look at them treated them as of no importance, so it really didn't matter; but poor Philip was made quite miserable—that is, almost miserable, since it was no longer possible for him to achieve that condition—and felt that it was really too bad of her to pull his leg in that way, for he was quite sure that she was the authoress of the plot.

Perhaps it was. Still, the jest was very feeble and harmless, and only modesty in its most exaggerated form could have been wounded by it. Not a soul in Brighthelmstone took the announcement of the Honorable Philip

Shelmerdine's arrival and positive reappearance that afternoon at all seriously.

But stay! In our chivalrous desire to excuse the Heroine, perhaps this statement is a little too general. There was one person, and just one person only, in Brighthelmstone who treated the handbill as a thing of consequence.

Mary, distributing her handbills along the King's Parade, assisted by her two companions in guilt and at least four other Olympians who had been specially coöpted for the purpose, while Philip, with his hands in his pockets, was trying to look supremely unconscious of the fact that his leg was being pulled frightfully, came upon a Bath Chair, a Sealskin Coat and a Himalayan Dust Spaniel.

"Are you feeling any *benefit* this morning, Lord Warlock? And please let me give you one of these. And you, Lady Adela, must take one, please. It is *so* important."

"Thank yah," said His Britannic Majesty's Ex-Ambassador to Persia. "If it's votes for women, I think they oughtn't to have 'em, although, mind you—benefit for the widow and five children of the late Joe McPherson—very praiseworthy object—shall be happy to subscribe a sovereign."

The Sealskin Coat, however, did not appear to look at the object in that Christian light. Having perused the handbill with an eye of cold disdain, Adela folded up the handbill neatly, and, without making any observation upon the merits of the case, placed it in her muff. But as soon as she returned to the Suffolk, she addressed an envelope to the Lady Shelmerdine of Potterhanworth, 88 Grosvenor Square, London, W., and therein enclosed, anonymously, of course, the announcement of the Honorable Philip's arrival and reappearance. A rather feeble thing to have done really, and hardly worthy of mention, except that it shows what human nature can achieve in a moment of reaction.

Philip was greeted effusively by the rest of his brothers in arms, who had now arrived at the Magnificent; and the Bride was introduced to them all. The report of her charms had been carried to them by Toddles and W. W., who were sealed of the tribe of her admirers already. And it had been agreed by the whole team that if she never did anything else, the fact that she had caused the finest inside right save one in the country to return to this important position after a lapse of four years, must ever count to her for grace.

Poor Philip was in a rather nervous state when he drove on to the ground in a brake with his ten companions and with Mary on the box-seat. That enterprising young woman had already elected herself to the important position of commander-in-chief of the famous team of amateurs, which contained no less than nine International players. But even this achievement was not exactly the fruit of self-assertion. She was one of those gifted people who instinctively, yet quite pleasantly and unobtrusively, take charge of everything and everybody. Already *persona gratissima* at the Suffolk; already saluted by the most dignified constables in Brighton; on terms of intimacy with the master of the longest pier—she had taken the Olympians under her wing in the most comprehensive manner.

The spectators came in their thousands because it was Saturday afternoon and the Albion were announced to play their full League team; and the Olympians with their nine International players were ever a great attraction. But the start was delayed ten minutes, and a great concourse was kept waiting because Mary had brought her kodak. She took charge of the Albion as well as their opponents; posing them for the camera, and appearing to know each of them by name, although she didn't really; but it was all done with the charm and the naïve assurance that had made her so famous with the public.

"Beg pardon, ma'am," said the Secretary and Manager; "don't like to hurry you, but the crowd is getting a bit restive."

"Oh, tell the band to play 'Rule Britannia,' and it will be all right," said Mary.

And in this her judgment was perfectly sound.

"Now, boys, look your best," said she. "All smile, please. Just imagine you have knocked out the Villa, which, of course, you will next Saturday, because I've made up my mind that you are going to, and I'm a proper mascot, as they know in the North. Not too broad, Joe Pierce, because of the plate. Ve-ry nice—ve-ry nice in-deed. Thank you, boys; and just see if you don't beat the Villa, although, of course, you are going to lose this afternoon."

So much for her handling of the democracy, which was brilliantly successful. The whole team were her humble servants to command, now that she had exercised her powers upon them. Her handling of the aristocracy—not that these idle class distinctions obtain upon the field of play—was equally happy. She was entirely responsible for the fact that the game began seventeen minutes late, but nobody seemed to mind particularly, "Rule Britannia" having been twice repeated.

A very good game it was, and a keenly critical crowd was vastly entertained. The famous inside right had not been forgotten, although the public memory is short as a rule. At first, in his new boots, he had, like a certain Biblical hero, to walk delicately; but he soon began to improve, and presently got on better than he had expected. Although he had not played football for four years, he was in fairly hard condition, as he took pretty regular exercise of one sort or another. Still, the pace was so hot at first that he felt it would be bound to kill him. But when at last he had got his second wind, and beautiful slow-stealing passes began to come his way from the famous center forward with whom he had shared many a triumph, the old magic seemed somehow to return, he began to enjoy the proceedings thoroughly, and so did the spectators.

The Albion scored a good goal quite early in the game, but just before half-time the center forward made the scores equal. Then the band played again; collecting-boxes were sent round the ground for the benefit of the widow and young family of the late Joe McPherson; and Mary herself took charge of one of them, and, of course, her box got twice as much as anybody else's, which was bound to be the case, since she looked so charming, and her way with the great British Public was very charming also.

Who was the lady wearing the ribbon of the Olympians, who was getting sixpences and shillings for her box, while the others had to be content with pence for the most part? Who was the lady with that wonderful way with her, whose handsome face—and it really did look handsome just now, for all that it was so square and sensible—was so familiar on picture-postcards and in illustrated papers?

The famous Miss Caspar from Drury Lane. No wonder her manner was so captivating. No wonder it was so pleasantly sure of itself, when all London had been times and again to watch her put on the Prince's slipper, and the Honorable P. Shelmerdine, the son of a lord and in his day a very fine player, and doing very well this afternoon, had been lucky enough to marry her.

Yes, the lady with the collecting-box was undoubtedly lending rare distinction to the proceedings. Sixpences and shillings and even half-crowns were raining into her box from the reserved enclosure. The widow and young family of the late Joe McPherson would, undoubtedly, gain very substantially from her efforts, as other deserving objects had done in the past and were likely to do in the future.

The rakish green hats of Horace and Johnny were well to the fore, and the fact that Mary couldn't possibly miss them cost their owners half-a-crown apiece. And Horace Allwright, as he proudly disbursed this sum, remembered that in the near future a benefit performance was going to be given at the Royal Italian Opera House, Blackhampton, for one who had served the public long and faithfully, but who now had fallen upon evil days.

"I say, Mary, old girl," said Horace, "that reminds me, we are giving a complimentary matinée at Blackhampton on Tuesday week for poor old Harry Merino—you remember poor old Harry—and you are such a great power in Blackhampton that I thought perhaps—"

"Why, of course," said Mary. "Half-a-crown, please, Horace. Yes, of course, put me down for 'Arcadee' and 'Nelson' and—now, do I ever forget?"

"No, you don't, old girl," said Horace Allwright humbly, and Johnny Dubosque echoed him.

"That's all right, then. And don't say another word to the man at the wheel, because we are losing money. Thank you, sir, so much. A *very* good cause—poor old Joe was one of the best."

How she knew that poor old Joe was one of the best it would be difficult to say. But, at least, she seemed able to convince the reserved enclosure that the case of Joe's widow and family was worthy of their charity, for when she delivered her box into the care of the secretary and manager soon after the game had re-started, that gentleman was astonished at the amount of money there was in it; moreover, he rubbed his hands with satisfaction, and paid a sincere and richly merited compliment to the celebrated lady from the Lane.

Mr. Philip in his new boots struggled manfully through the second half of the game, although there was precious little skin left on his toes by this time; and he wondered how he was going to live to the end, since there didn't seem to be a breath left in him. But something of the old magic had come back. If he could only kick a goal for his side, he would feel that his life had not been lived in vain.

As luck would have it, this desire was gratified. Still, this may not be altogether surprising, having regard to the fact that every movement of those mutilated toes engaged the sympathetic interest of a mascot mighty in the North, and in the South also, if it came to that. There were only about ten minutes to play; the score was still one all, when another of those beautiful slow-stealing passes came from the center forward, and Philip, knowing that it was now or never, drew the bow at a venture in the inspired way he did in his prime. And somehow he happened to time his effort at the psychological instant,—just as a stalwart son of Caledonia knocked him right into the middle of next week.

That is how the Albion came to lose the match. Yet the result didn't matter really; very spirited and skillful play had been shown by both sides, there was nothing at stake, and a good cause had prospered. But Philip was the proudest and happiest man in Brighthelmstone as he staggered to the dressing-room with his poor feet, and knowing full well that he would hardly be able to walk for a fortnight.

CHAPTER XXIII
IN WHICH GRANDMAMMA RENEWS HERS

WHEN Philip and Mary returned to the King's Parade with their inmost thoughts centered upon a dish of tea, a great surprise awaited them. The sitting-room overlooking the sea was in the occupation of no less a person than His Britannic Majesty's Ex-Ambassador to Persia. He had come, it appeared, to thank Grandmamma personally for the loan of her apparatus, and to commemorate the amount of good it had already done the complaint from which they suffered in common.

It happened that Grandmamma, like other old ladies who have moved in the world, could talk to a lord as well as most people if she happened to be in the humor. Well, she had had a pretty good nap; the cap-with-the-Siddons'-lace was as straight as you please; and she had a distinct recollection of having met the Ex-Ambassador at Knebworth somewhere about the year 1881.

Long before Philip, accompanied by Mary, returned in his unconventional footballing costume, these two interesting persons were getting on like a house on fire. The past was reconstructed and repeopled; the present was deplored, and, alas! abused not a little. Mrs. Cathcart had known Mr. Gladstone, Mr. Disraeli—whom she couldn't abide!—Mr. Dickens, Mr. Thackeray, Lord Tennyson, Mr. Bright, and Garibaldi. Comparisons are invidious, but where are the persons of that type nowadays?

Lord Warlock entirely agreed with the goddaughter of Bean. Alas, the world had fallen upon evil days indeed!

"But I think, ma'am, you have a devilish sensible granddaughter, if I may say so."

Grandmamma hoped her granddaughter was sensible, although to her mind it seemed that she had not married very prudently.

No brains, certainly, agreed my lord—speaking of the young chap, of course—but perhaps a young chap was just as well without 'em, provided his income was large enough to supply the deficiency.

However, it was more a Question of Principle to the mind of Grandmamma. And a Question of Principle is, of course, a great matter. The stage and the peerage had so little in common that they were best kept apart. Not, to be sure, that Grandmamma was blind to the worldly advantages, but then, to one who had played Lady Macbeth to John Peter Kendall, worldly advantages were not everything.

Mary and Philip undoubtedly interrupted an agreeable *tête-à-tête*. But the Ex-Ambassador shook hands with them both, and informed Mary once more how devilish obliged he was for the improvement that had already been wrought in his rheumatism. Mary was delighted to hear that, of course; and she rang for more tea and ordered *heaps* of hot buttered cakes; and Pa was so genial that this might never have been the creature who had stolen a march on Adela.

Mr. Philip, it must be admitted, was not very conversational. Even in the most favorable circumstances he was a silent young man. But Mary could talk enough for two, or enough for twenty if it came to that, being one of those gifted young women who are never at a loss in any society. Yet she was tactful, of course, with this Grecian gift—yes, it is a Grecian gift, you young ladies of Newnham and Girton; and if you possess this valuable faculty to the degree that Mary did, be like her and never, never abuse it.

The Tactful Young Madam hoped that Lord Warlock would excuse their unconventional attire. They had been playing football for the benefit of the widow and five young children of the late Joe McPherson, and ten thousand people had been present and quite a substantial sum was likely to be raised, and if Lord Warlock would be so kind as to give her the sovereign he had promised her for the Fund she would have great pleasure in forwarding it to the Treasurer, and she was sure the Treasurer would have equal pleasure in receiving it, because the Cause was so Deserving.

Pa paid up there and then, like a fine old Irish gentleman and a sportsman to boot; and Mary promised to send on the receipt as soon as she received it; and my lord said the receipt was of no consequence; and Mary, with her square and sensible face, said a receipt was always of consequence; not that she contradicted Pa at all rudely, you know, as we fear another young person has been known to do on occasion.

She then explained that their side had won the match by two goals to one, and that the winning goal had been scored by Philip; and my lord remarked that a devilish good game was polo, and it was a great pity we had allowed the Cup to go to America, and we must send a good team and plenty of ponies and get it back again; in which the Siddons'-cap-of-real-lace concurred with great spirit, and affirmed her conviction that there had been negligence somewhere.

"Oh, we shall just muddle along until Uncle Jonathan annexes us, and then we shall begin to wake up a bit, I daresay."

And everybody laughed loudly, of course, at the caustic Ambassadorial Humor.

But it wasn't polo they had been playing, says little Miss Newnham, with her passion for exactitude. Of course it wasn't, my dear. Then why didn't Mary say so? Her Tact again, my dear. It always bores a real live ex-ambassador to have to stand corrected; and football is so plebeian that polo sounds nicer; and it really didn't matter a straw, so there was no use in being tediously literal, was there?

You don't see the point of the argument, and you still think, my dear, it was Mary's duty to make it clear that the game was football. Sorry not to agree with *you*, Miss Newnham; but we are sure we shall have the sanction of all parents and guardians when we lay down the axiom that it is a chief part of the whole duty of Woman never to bore an ambassador.

Had Mary been tediously literal she would probably not have received an invitation to Hurlingham any afternoon she cared to come during the season, which she promptly accepted with becoming gratitude. And then, before the Ex-Ambassador could take up his hat and rise from the sofa, she had asked the important question, Could Lord Warlock be so *very* kind as to give her advice how to get Philip into Parliament?

There was a question for you! Give *her* advice, mark you, young ladies. There was a great deal in that. The Ex-Ambassador fixed his monocle, of course, with a little pardonable magniloquence of bearing, like any other ex-ambassador would have done; looked about as wise as you make 'em, and said in the sharp dry manner that he had really copied from his father who had copied it from Mr. Rogers, although that was a secret that lay with him in his grave—and what did the Ex-Ambassador say?

He said the best way to get into Parliament is to see that you keep out of it....

How very deep and subtle; quite worthy of Mr. Punch at his best, say all parents and guardians.

We can't see the point of the reply, say the dreadfully literal young ladies of Newnham and Girton.

Well, if you really can't, my dears, it is not for us to attempt to explain it.

Anyhow, that was the Ambassadorial reply; and real Tact—the genuine guaranteed article—in the person of Mistress Mary was delighted with this brilliant *mot*; and the real lace of Siddons immensely admired its *esprit*, and said quite audibly to the crochet-work antimacassar "that it was worthy of dear Dicky Milnes"; and the Ex-Ambassador, still feeling quite comfortable on the sofa, in spite of the fact that the springs were broken and that the stuffing was distributed so unevenly, thought he might just as well stay another five minutes.

There can be no doubt that the extension of the visit was entirely due to Mary's tact. And now, young ladies, let us see the use that she made of it.

"If only there would be a vacancy at Blackhampton I think I could get him in myself, because I really think I have got Blackhampton in my pocket."

"A very right and proper place in which to keep a borough; it was in our time, Mrs. Cathcart, eh?"

The Siddons' cap and the inheritor of the Rogers tradition had this delectable morsel all to themselves. The brain of Mary the Tactful was much too busy marshalling its battalions, and Mr. Philip was far too much interested in hot buttered tea-cake, which he had certainly earned, to be able to follow the conversation except at a very respectful distance. Therefore the continued *esprit* of my lord was like to have gone unhonored save for Granny, who could have imagined Sydney Smith, etc.

So, after all, it was really as much due to the Siddons' cap that the five minutes grew into ten; and this further extension was rather important, since Mary was busy posing the mighty problem how could she get this absentee Irish landlord, who was bound by the nature of the case to be a Vandeleurite, to play the game of a perfectly ferocious Balsquithian.

"You see, Lord Warlock, I want my Philip to go into Parliament, but we don't know anybody who has got any influence with Mr. Balsquith, because all our friends are on the other side."

A very nicely calculated candor, Miss Mary; well might the Ex-Ambassador present a picture of amiable cynicism.

"Seems to me, then, you had better apply to the other party."

"Oh, no, Lord Warlock. My Philip is nothing like clever enough to be a Vandeleurite."

Rather sacrificing her lord, though, wasn't she, on the altar of high diplomacy? Not that Mr. Philip minded that particularly. Hot buttered tea-cake was of far more consequence than anything that had transpired up to the present.

The Ex-Ambassador was constrained to feel that the ambitious young woman's reasoning was sound. The young hussy then proceeded to draw her next card out of the pack, and it wasn't a very bad one, either.

"You see, Lord Warlock, I am so keen for my Philip to go into politics, as I want people to say that the best day's work he ever did was when he married me."

There was only one reply for an old diplomatist to make to this engaging candor. It is hardly necessary to say that no time was lost in making it.

How did Mary, who is really too pushing to be quite nice, in my opinion, receive the obviously insincere compliment that was paid to her? says our little friend Miss Newnham. She didn't say a word, my dear, but she blushed quite charmingly—at least, the Ex-Ambassador thought she did—and then that absolutely direct glance of about two thousand candle-power came right at the noble earl, who proceeded to register on the tablets of his worldly wise old mind the following pearl of wisdom: No Wonder The Young Fools Marry 'Em Nowadays.

"So you want to get him into Parliament, do you—as a Rag?" mused the old cynic.

"Dear Lord Warlock, if you would only give me a little advice, I am really so ignorant!"

There was just room for two persons on the decrepit sofa that had the honor of holding my lord. Would it bear the weight of both of 'em? was another poser for Mary the Tactful. She would risk it, anyhow; and so she sat down beside the Ex-Ambassador in a charmingly impulsive manner, and said, "Dear Lord Warlock, do help me," and very nearly slew one who had grown old in the world with her good gray eyes.

It may almost be laid down as an axiom that ex-ambassadors are pretty deep as a rule. This one was certainly not an exception. Not only did his dark and self-contained appearance suggest considerable guile, but this picturesque impression was amply confirmed by the fascinating curves of his intellect. In fine, my lords and gentlemen, His Britannic Majesty's Ex-Ambassador to Persia was a long way from being a fool.

Therefore he made no immediate reply to Mary the Tactful. But the Pushful Young Hussy—as every young married woman should be, my dear Miss Newnham—knew perfectly well that she had given the fellow-occupant of the sofa to think. As a matter of fact, the fellow-occupant thought considerable, and somewhat to this tenor.

I am not very pleased with Vandeleur just now. He as good as promised me that vacant Thistle, but he gave it to Blougram instead, who, of course, has not rendered one-tenth of my services to the Empire. Then this young fool is the eldest son of an old fool who takes himself far too seriously—an old fool who has jobbed his way into unmerited favor, and has done as much as anybody, outside the perfectly appalling Front Bench, to ruin the party. Well, I owe Vandeleur a grudge; I can't abide pompous mediocrity; I'm feeling rather mischievous just now with this ill-tempered girl o' mine left on my hands, when she ought to have been settled five years ago; and if the successor to Van's very last and very worst creation goes over lock, stock and barrel to the Rag, Tag and Bobtails, legs are going to be pulled pretty badly all round, eh?"

We hope the reasoning of the noble lord is clear to all parents and guardians. Certainly it is a little advanced for the junior members of the congregation. We have done our humble best to make it as lucid as possible, but the mental processes of an Ex-Ambassador call for the very nicest skill on the part of our Pegasus, who was never a very agile beast, at his best, and age don't improve him.

Mary the Tactful waited quite a minute for the Fellow-Occupant to break the silence. And then into little pieces the silence was shattered.

"I don't say I've any influence with Balsquith, but I might throw out a hint to Huffham and MacMurdo and the other Rag, Tag and Bobtail wire pullers that your man would like to stand for 'em, and a very able man, too."

Tactful Mary was breathless with gratitude. But not for a moment did her statesmanlike grasp desert her.

"Some large manufacturing town—Leeds or Bootle, or Sheffield, or Blackhampton, where they'd remember my Cinderella, and where I've presented medals, and where I've sung at concerts, when they've brought home T'Coop. If Free Trade and I can't get him in in any of those places, where they know a Cinderella when they see one—"

The granddaughter of the goddaughter of Edward Bean burst into a peal of laughter.

There was the grim light of Humor also in the ambassadorial eye.

"Best thing you can do, Mrs. Shelmerdine," said Worldly Wisdom, "is to see that your young chap writes a nice sensible letter to Balsquith, stating his views clearly in as few words as he can; and in the meantime I'll sow a few myself, and get Huffham or MacMurdo to meet him at lunch at the Helicon; and if at the next bye-election one Vandeleur don't get his leg pulled, I'm better fitted to eat Thistles than to wear 'em."

Even Mary the Tactful, whose knowledge of the world was so immense, hardly appreciated the full flavor of the latter remark; but what she did appreciate, and quite keenly, too, was the enormous importance of those that had preceded it.

She didn't overdo her gratitude because ex-ambassadors are not at all partial to Fuss. She thanked my lord very simply and sincerely; but she let the good gray eyes do most of the work, and very charmingly they did it. A very sensible girl, who will make a good wife for anybody, and I only wish that insolent wench of mine had got half her brains, thought the Ambassadorial One. Not that he said so to Mary the Tactful; although, strictly between ourselves, young ladies of Newnham and Girton, she wouldn't have minded very much if he had.

Lord Warlock took his leave at last, having passed quite an agreeable hour, whereas he had but expected a formal perfunctory ten minutes. It had been indeed a pleasure to meet Mrs. Cathcart again; and we have seen what an impression the granddaughter had made upon the old diplomatist. Yes, he assured the latter, a word in season should reach the chiefs of the Party. It was rash to make promises, but he hoped and believed—particularly as the Rags were always on the look-out for young men of family in order to redress the balance a bit—Mr. Philip might find himself in the midst of a bye-election in the not distant future.

This was imparted to Mary in strict confidence, while she conducted the visitor downstairs. And when the young minx had sped my lord over the doorstep with her picture-postcard smile, she came up the stairs again, two at a time, with the air of one who has really done something clever.

"And now, Phil-ipp," said she, "you must go at once and have a nice warm bath; and I will go to the chemist's and get something for those poor feet."

CHAPTER XXIV
IS OF A POLITICAL NATURE

GRANNY'S fortnight at Brighton was so successful that it ran to a month. In the latter part of the period Philip and Mary paid several flying visits to the metropolis to see if the little flat in Knightsbridge was coming up to expectations. The furniture also had to be considered, and a very pleasant occupation it was to collect the household gods.

Everything in the new house delighted them; the color of the walls, the light in the pictures, the hang of the curtains, the disposition of the chairs. It was about the first week in April when they started housekeeping for themselves. They had found a very warm and cozy little nest, rather high up perhaps, yet a nest is none the worse for that as a rule. It overlooked the park in which the birds were building, and in which Philip, who had turned over an entirely new leaf, used to ride before breakfast.

Mary's first cross in her new life was that she couldn't accompany him. But she had never been on a horse in her life; and she very much regretted now that this branch of her education had been neglected. They must be pals in everything. Wherever he went and whatever he did, she must be at his side—that is, if he wanted her, and she was quite sure he did.

As became a very practical-minded young woman, she soon came to grips with this important subject. It was one day after lunch, while the world was still seeming a truly magnificent place to be in, and life still appeared a truly noble and glorious invention.

"Phil-ipp, there is only one cloud so far."

"What is it, old girl?"

"I want to ride, Phil-ipp, and I don't know how. I think I shall learn. Come with me and order a habit, although at a really economical shop, because I'm not earning no money and I've broken all my contracts and this is going to be a dreadful Expense."

Philip was delighted and praised her pluck; but, in strict confidence, young ladies of Newnham and Girton, she didn't exactly overflow with that valuable commodity when she made her début a week later at the school. Her second and third appearances were hardly more inspiring; indeed, she had never felt so uncomfortable, so nervous, so hopelessly incompetent in the whole course of a life which had been a brilliant success so far. But she stuck to her resolve with the whole-hearted determination that goes with her type of countenance; and ere long virtue began to reap its reward.

It was a very proud moment when, after several weeks of travail, she ventured forth into the Row with her Philip, about a quarter-past eight of a summer's morning. Philip felt awfully proud of her, for, making due allowance for a little inward trepidation which was uncommonly well concealed, she really did very well indeed. She vowed, moreover, though in no spirit of vainglory, that she meant soon to do much better.

Friends of the Family had shaken their heads, and were shaking them still, over the Unfortunate Occurrence, but at present the glamour had shown no signs of wearing thin. Mary had definitely retired from the theater, except for the promised appearance at Harry Merino's benefit, which had yet to take place, but in the most whole-hearted way she was devoting herself to Philip and his interests. It was her ambition "to be a pal in everything." The sitting of a horse was only one instance of her determination to live up to her ideal.

An Ex-Ambassador had asked her to call in Mount Street. No time was lost in taking him at his word. Moreover, she chose a day and hour when the old diplomatist was accessible. And her recent study of the art of equitation came in uncommonly useful, inasmuch that without much difficulty she contrived "to keep him up to the bit." That is to say, about ten days after her visit Philip received an invitation to lunch at the Helicon, to meet a chief wire-puller of the party to which the Ex-Ambassador did not belong. It is not every young married woman of limited social experience who would have been able to manage it.

To be quite candid, Sir Joseph Huffham, Bart., M. P., was not exactly overpowered by the sense of Mr. Philip's ability. To that shrewd and stern judge of mankind, the son and heir of that old fool Shelmerdine was very much what one would have expected him to be. Except that he was not pompous. On the contrary, there was a most agreeable modesty about the young chap. It was evidently sincere, and as such was entitled to respect. As far as promise was concerned, though there was doubtless a good deal of it—a worldly-wise man had said so—whatever he might attain to in the way of performance would be in the distant future.

What had Warlock in his mind? was really the question of questions for Sir Joseph Huffham, Bart., M. P. What Machiavellian subtlety lurked in the bringing forward of this very dark horse for the purpose of helping a party in which Warlock was not interested? What private axe had he to grind? To be sure, there was that little business of the vacant Thistle, which all the world and his wife had smiled over. Then there was also the fact that this not particularly bright young man had disappointed the expectations of two families. What game was the old Jesuit playing? was the question that Sir Joseph felt constrained to ask.

Sir Joseph found the question by no means easy to answer, and we must confess that we share his difficulty. It would be idle, my lords and gentlemen, for us to pretend to illuminate the official prescience. But candidly, we feel that the question might have been addressed to young Mrs. Philip without impropriety, although, of course, Sir Joseph could not be expected to know that, and he would have thought it ridiculous had anyone ventured to make the suggestion. Things don't happen in that way, he would have said.

Maybe, Sir Joseph; yet perchance in that case you would have affirmed but half a truth. It takes a pretty bold man these days to say exactly how things do happen, Monsieur Bergson seems to think.

Still, Sir Joseph certainly thought it was piquant that the son of S. of P. should desire to help the Party. His qualifications for public life appeared to be rather obscure, but being the eldest son of his father he was not without a face value for the enemy.

"And so, Mr. Shelmerdine," said the illustrious man, smiling over the club claret, "you think, with your wife's assistance, you might be able to win a seat like South-West Blackhampton for the party of progress."

"My wife is sure she could win it for me," was the answer of Philip.

It was not, perhaps, the answer to be expected from a champion of the democracy; and the illustrious man looked rather quizzically across the table at his host. Were he and his party going to have their legs pulled in company with Van and the other side? Never trust an Irishman on principle, was one of Sir Joseph's axioms; and in this case he rather felt like living up to it.

All the same, the exigencies of the situation called for a man somewhat out of the ordinary for South-West Blackhampton. At present that large and important industrial constituency was represented by a man of independent mind who owed allegiance to none. The power of his personality had carried him to the top of the poll in a three-cornered contest, in spite of the fact that he had an official Rag and an official Wagger, able men both, against him.

Good, sound, conventional candidates had failed against this Rawhead and Bloodybones. It was just possible that the husband of a favorite actress, and a famous footballer to boot, might be successful where his betters might fail. That, at least, was the local opinion.

"I presume, Mr. Shelmerdine," said Sir Joseph Huffham, "in the event of your being adopted as a candidate for South-West Blackhampton, you would have no objection to signing a—er—" Sir Joseph paused while he took a type-written document from his pocket-book and adjusted his pince-nez—"a football league form for the Blackhampton Rovers?"

Mr. Shelmerdine was quite prepared to do that.

"And of playing for them occasionally, I presume, if your services were called upon?"

Mr. Shelmerdine had no objection to doing that, either, although he was rather short of practice these days.

"I am informed, Mr. Shelmerdine, that you kicked three goals against Scotland in an International match."

With excellent modesty the young man admitted this impeachment.

"Well, I think I am entitled to say, Mr. Shelmerdine," said Sir Joseph, who was himself a pretty shrewd Lancastrian, "if you can kick three goals against Liverpool or Manchester City in an important League match, you are very likely to be returned at the top of the poll."

Very simply and seriously, and quite sincerely, Mr. Shelmerdine promised to do his best in this matter, and that when the time came, if South-West Blackhampton did him the honor of adopting him as their candidate, he would go into strict training for the purpose.

Sir Joseph had the reputation of being the possessor of a sense of humor, and the Ex-Ambassador had a few ideas also upon that recondite subject; but each of these gentlemen smiled very warily at the other, as though he was not quite certain whether it would be safe in the circumstances to allow his mobile fancy to play around that which had rather the appearance of a jest on the surface. Had they not mistrusted one another so sorely, they might have been tempted to do so; but the odd thing was that the prospective candidate for South-West Blackhampton respected their *bona fides* so immensely that he remained a perfect image of gravity.

"I will do my best, sir, to kick three goals against Liverpool or Manchester City," said the young man as he shook hands and took his leave.

"Then I think you may be returned to Parliament," said the shrewd Lancastrian cordially; "that is, if you never hold a meeting without having your wife on the platform; and you let her do most of the talking, you know."

It was frankness, certainly, on the part of Sir Joseph Huffham, Bart., M.P.; but that illustrious man owed much of his eminence to the fact that he had a pretty sound working knowledge of things in general.

"I will certainly do that, sir," said the young man.

Whereupon he thanked Sir Joseph and the Ex-Ambassador with great sincerity, and went his way along Pall Mall; and as he did this he was just the happiest young man in all the great Metropolis. It was a genuine inspiration that Mary should make the speeches. He would attend to the goal-kicking department all right. He would go into strict training, knock off tobacco, lead the life of an anchorite. And when he found himself in Parliament as a full-blown Rag, he would be able to say that she had done it all.

Hitherto Mr. Philip had not been encumbered with anything so superfluous as political convictions. He had known in a dim kind of way that the friends of his youth had been Waggers. Without the Waggers, he had always been given to understand there would have been no turn-up with the Boers in South Africa. He had borne a humble part in that little affair, along with the rest of his friends; and the best he could say for it was that he had found it rather an overrated amusement. But without the Waggers, so he understood, there would not have been fair play for everybody.

However, this was the only good thing he knew about the Waggers. His father was a Wagger, of course, like everybody else's father was; but if you have quarrelled with your father, there is all the less reason to stick to the same school of political thought. But Mary it was who had really converted him, and had made him go into Parliament. She declared herself to be an absolutely ferocious Rag-Tag-and-Bobtail, and that, of course, in the present state of the domestic firmament, was quite enough for Mr. Philip.

The Rags, as Mary expounded their faith, were the party of Progress and the friends of the People. And now that he was enlisted in their ranks, he felt it behoved him to live up to their exalted principles. Therefore he gave a shilling to the crossing-sweeper at the bottom of Saint James's Street, and, like a true democrat, proceeded on foot to the little nest in Knightsbridge, instead of going like the son of a lord in a taxi.

Mary was buried in a delightfully comfortable chair with her toes on the fender. She was also reading a novel; and out of our love for her we must really withhold the name of the author.

... No, young ladies of Newnham and Girton, the name of the author was not Monsieur Anatole France.

"I've done it, old girl," said Mr. Philip, bursting in upon her and saluting her, of course, in the manner ordained by custom for newly-married people. "I really think they are going to take me on."

Strictly speaking, young man, you had not done it. It was Mary who had done all the doing so far; although, of course, you could hardly be expected to realize that.

"Oh, how splendid!"

"Yes, old girl; and old Sir Joseph Thingamy—nice old boy—says you are to attend all the meetings and make most of the speeches, and I'm to sign a League form for Blackhampton Rovers and kick three goals against Liverpool, and everything will be as right as rain."

"Why, of course it will, Phil-ipp, when I've got dear old Blackhampton in my pocket."

And Mary flung away her novel, and rose with the light of battle in her eye in order to confirm this startling announcement.

A general election was expected in October. The head office said things must be put in train at once. Communications had, of course, to pass between the constituency and Westminster, but within a month Mr. Philip had received an invitation from the Chief Tribesmen of South-West Blackhampton to come forth and make the acquaintance with his views.

Then it was that Mr. Philip found himself in a bit of a funk. The fact was that he hadn't any views—at least, any views to speak about. Party of progress; government of the People, by the People, for the People; greatest good of the greatest number, and so forth. That was all he knew, and you couldn't very well make a speech out of that, could you?

With this, however, Mary didn't quite agree. She seemed to think you could. She had been reading up the subject lately. Therefore she sat down at once, pen in hand, and began to collect her ideas upon the subject.

In common with other ready-witted people, she had the useful faculty of being fluent on paper. By lunch-time she had covered ten pages of foolscap, writing on one side of the paper only; and after lunch, when over the cigarettes and coffee she read the result of her labors aloud to the future member for South-West Blackhampton, the young man found it hard to repress his enthusiasm.

"I shall have 'em absolutely stiff," said he; "that is, if I can only remember it all. But I say, old girl, what if they begin to ask questions?"

"Tell them, Phil-ipp, that you believe in Mr. Balsquith; and that anything he votes for you'll vote for, because you know that *he* can't go wrong."

"Yes, that's all right, old girl, but a chap is expected to have a bit of a mind of his own, ain't he?"

"Dear, no—pray *why* should he have?" And this worldly wise young wife started on cigarette the second, we are rather sorry to say, because one should suffice after lunch even for a young married woman. Still, the circumstances were exceptional.

"Trust Mr. Balsquith, and South-West Blackhampton will trust you. Now start learning your speech, like a good boy; and you must repeat it to me word for word every morning from memory, so that you'll be all right on the night and absolutely word perfect."

As an instance of Providence in one of its less atrabilious humors, it befell that Philip was invited to meet the local committee in the evening following the one in which Mary was to appear at the Royal Italian Opera House for the benefit of Harry Merino. Thus they were able to stay together at the best hotel in Blackhampton, and to feel that they were killing, as it were, two birds with a single stone.

It was perfectly true that at Blackhampton the name of Mary Caspar ranked high with the population. It was in the largest type on every hoarding; her portrait appeared in the window of every other shop; her wonderful smile that wouldn't come off was to be seen on countless picture-postcards; an illustrated interview with the general favorite was printed in the *Blackhampton Courier*.

When she walked down Market Street to do a little shopping on the afternoon of her arrival in the borough, she caused almost as much commotion as if she had been Royalty itself. And in the opinion of her escort, a very nice-looking, well-grown and well-groomed young man in white spats and a blue suiting, the last word in neatness, and a bowler hat, of course the last word of fashion, she was indeed the Queen of Blackhampton. Moreover, a large percentage of the passers-by concurred with the nice-looking young man in so thinking.

Yes, she was the acknowledged Queen of Blackhampton; in the eyes of the passers-by the fact was stated. It was perfectly true that she had got this constituency in her pocket; and Blackhampton, although hardly aware of the fact, was mightily proud to be there.

They came in their thousands to welcome her back to that sphere of life she ought never to have deserted. Their reception almost brought tears to her eyes, it was so spontaneous, so hearty, and so genuine. The Royal Italian Opera House could have been filled ten times over; not, of course, that this was due to Mary alone. Other stars were giving their services; and Harry Merino, upon whom evil times had fallen, was as good a comedian as ever colored his nose and delighted the world with irresistible natural humor.

It was at the Royal at Blackhampton that she had really begun her great career. Blackhampton had been the making of her, said Mr. Byles, the famous Lessee and Manager of the Royal, and that great man was accustomed to deal with hard facts. Blackhampton believed it, anyway; and Mary believed it also. At least, she confessed as much to Mr. Byles, while the chest of the lessee grew so large that it seemed that his watch-chain of twenty-two carat gold must really break from its moorings.

"Polly, my gal, I'm proud o' you!"—there was deep emotion in the manly voice of the Lessee and Manager; and if "the Young Pup" had not been present, it is most likely that Mr. Byles would have hugged the future peeress publicly.

Yes, they were very hearty, genuine people at Blackhampton. The Principal Girl of three Royal pantomimes was to them an imperishable memory. In the divine order of womanhood the Queen of England ranked first in their estimation; Mary Caspar ranked second; and the third place was reserved for the Duchess of Dumbarton, although local opinion was rather averse from the peerage merely as such.

It was probable that one such as Mr. Philip would find a difficult row to hoe in Blackhampton. They hadn't much use for frills as a general thing. If the young man was going to stand for Blackhampton, it was by no means clear that those white spats were not an error of judgment. But the general opinion was that even a future hereditary legislator might be returned for Blackhampton if he happened to be Mary Caspar's husband, and that he signed a league form for the Rovers, and kicked a few goals against Aston Villa.

He was a nice-looking young gentleman certainly, said feminine Blackhampton; a little too fine for the district, perhaps, and yet they were by no means sure of that. Good looks, a good tailor and easy, natural manners tell even at Blackhampton among the ladies; and even there, as in more sophisticated places, public opinion is susceptible to their judgments.

Alderman Slocock, J. P., the leading Rag statesman for twenty miles around, presided at the meeting of the executive committee at the Gladstone Club. The proceedings were of a strictly private character; ladies were not admitted; Mary could not be present; and in consequence The Pup longed for his coffin even before the proceedings started.

Alderman Slocock made a very long speech from the chair. The prospective candidate would be given every opportunity to express his views at length; but before coming to that part of the programme, Alderman Slocock, a master-hairdresser, with no fewer than twenty-four shops spread over the district, spoke for nearly an hour.

It was not a very opportune beginning, since the longer the master-hairdresser went on, the more intense grew Mr. Philip's desire for a speedy burial; moreover, the other members of the committee were growing decidedly restless. But at last came the fateful moment when the Candidate was called upon to express his views; and then arose the question for gods and men, would the Candidate be able to remember them?

For three solid weeks, every morning and every night, from memory had he repeated to Mary his speech. There must be no doubt as to his ability to cope with this great ordeal. When he entered the Gladstone Club he would have wagered that he was absolutely word perfect; but as soon as he got on his legs he was paralyzed with the knowledge that he couldn't remember a syllable.

To begin with, his throat was so terribly dry that he was bound to have recourse to a liquid aid to eloquence before he "could come to the horses." But there were broad-minded men and advanced thinkers on the Executive Committee who rather approved this weakness because it showed that the Candidate was human like themselves, and they thought none the worse of him for it. On the other hand, there were representatives of Little Bethel in this august assembly who deplored the Candidate's early recourse to whisky and water.

Mr. Chairman and Gentlemen, began the wretched Philip, in a thin, small voice. Oh, joy! at the instance of those familiar words the speech suddenly began to flow automatically into his mind. Members of the Gladstone Club, Electors of Blackhampton—the cunning young minx had said that this style of address was bound to sound well in the ears of the Committee—I have followed with the closest attention and I may say with deep admiration, the speech from Alderman Slocock to which we have just had the pleasure of listening. I cannot understand how it is, gentlemen, that having a man like Alderman Slocock in your midst, you should go outside your fine old city, of which I am sure you must be awfully proud, to look for a man worthy to represent it in Parliament. (Loud applause which bucked up the candidate considerably.)

Let us pay no idle compliment to the authoress of the speech, but we are by no means clear that the young madam did not know more about the rules of the game than augurs well for the peace of mind of the coming generation which may have to cope with her sex on the green benches.

Certainly this felicitous opening seemed to put the candidate on good terms with his audience. Things began to go very well. The voice was good; the manner, of course, what you would expect from the Twin Brethren; the matter was sound so far as it went, and very wisely it did not go further than amiable generalities. He was the son of a lord undoubtedly, but it was clear that he was much above the average of his class.

The end of his ordeal was not yet, however. Alderman Slocock had a few questions to ask.

Would the Candidate be good enough to enlighten the Committee as to the nature of his views upon the subject of Free Trade?

Sir, I shall be most happy, said the Candidate, smiling graciously. Gentlemen, my views on the subject of Free Trade are those of Mr. Balsquith, and it is a matter upon which I trust his judgment implicitly.

The Committee was much gratified by this statesmanlike reply.

And the question of the House of Lords? said Alderman Slocock. The Committee would be happy to have the Candidate's views upon that vexed subject.

The views of the Candidate in respect of the House of Lords were those of Mr. Balsquith; that also was a subject upon which he trusted Mr. Balsquith's judgment implicitly.

This answer was equally successful; and as it did duty for all the questions that followed, the Candidate was guilty of nothing that was likely to efface the highly favorable effect he had already created. Therefore he was able to return to the best hotel in Blackhampton reasonably secure in the conviction that he was about to be chosen as the official representative of the Rags.

Of course he would be, he was promptly informed by Mary, who was sitting up for him, if he had remembered his words.

"Fact is, old girl," confided Mr. Philip, "I knew I'd got 'em fixed up before I'd got half through my bally speech."

"Why, of course, Phil-ipp, you were bound to have."

And she was far too good a sportswoman to remind the vainglorious orator that it was not his speech at all. But don't let us praise her too much.

For the simple fact was that it pleased her mightily to think that it really was his speech that had carried the day, and that she had nothing whatever to do with it. Moreover, she was perfectly willing for him to believe that it was his speech; and certainly, so high had success lifted her lord just now that it didn't really seem very difficult for him to do so. And for our own poor part, we have never been able to determine which phenomenon is the more curious: whether Man should plume himself beyond his deserts at the expense of Woman or whether Woman should derive a keen pleasure from aiding and abetting him in the deception.

Howbeit, so deep was the impression that Mr. Philip Shelmerdine's signal ability, in combination with his air of manly sincerity and straightforwardness, made upon the Committee, that no time was lost in inviting him to stand as a Rag, Tag and Bobtail for South-West Blackhampton.

CHAPTER XXV
IS VICTORIAN IN THE BEST SENSE

IN Grosvenor Square, at this period, rose-color was not the prevailing hue. The Proconsul had declined to attend the wedding. Moreover, he had given Mr. Philip clearly to understand that Mrs. Philip would not be *persona gratissima* in Grosvenor Square. The attitude was perfectly "regular" in the circumstances; all the same, it hardly increased the common stock of human amenity. And he was quite an affectionate father, even if a somewhat despotic one, which, after all, is not an unexpected trait in a middle-aged gentleman who has made a great success of the art of governing others.

The attitude of the Proconsul is hardly one to commend to parents and guardians in general. And unfortunately Mother upheld the Proconsul in his frowardness. She, too, as had so many Colthursts of Suffolk before her, formed the fatal habit of governing others. And she, too, having been thwarted in a pet design, and moreover, having had to submit to a pretty shrewd buffet from the venerable relative of The Person, was inclined to behave with unwisdom.

It is a great pity that Grosvenor Square has to be shown in this light. Both Father and Mother ought really to have known so very much better. It was really very wrong; and they made themselves rather miserable into the bargain.

Mother thought Father ought to have been firmer. Father thought that Mother ought to have kept clear of Bedford Gardens, and all would have been well. Mother thought that Father's handling of the whole matter was hardly worthy of a Proconsul. Father was grieved that Agatha should talk in that way, since it would be idle to pretend that she had shown her usual Tact.

Nevertheless, there was one aspect of the affair that really astonished both of them immensely. It was the attitude taken up by a much-injured man and a thwarted father-in-law when they ventured to condole with him, and perhaps incidentally to obtain a little balm for their own wounded feelings.

Father and Mother were frankly amazed that their standpoint had to forego the sanction of His Britannic Majesty's Ambassador to Persia.

"Fact is, Shelmerdine," said my lord, "the young fool has done a dashed sight better for himself than by marrying this girl of mine."

Mother was amazed at such levity proceeding from such a quarter; and rather pointedly she said so.

"We must look facts in the face," said my lord robustly. "She is an uncommonly able young woman, and one of these days you'll remember that I've said so."

"I don't think I like ability in women," said Mother.

Oh, Mother! And you, by common consent, one of the ablest women in Grosvenor Square and its environs.

"It's a useful thing to keep in the house, though," said the Ex-Ambassador.

Still, Mother was not in the least resigned to what she considered an exhibition of cynicism.

"One is really surprised at *you*, Lord Warlock—you who know the world so well."

And yet it would be hardly safe to assume that Mother was wholly sincere in her admonition of this elderly diplomatist. She didn't subscribe to his ignoble point of view; she never could and never would subscribe to it; but it would hardly be safe to assume that Mother was seriously displeased that a man of such penetration should entertain it.

Still, she had to labor the Victorian Attitude a little in order to cope with one so unexpected.

"If only she had been a—"

The Ex-Ambassadorial chuckle brought Mother up short.

"We shall see what we shall see, dear lady."

Mother wished my lord would not be so cryptic. All the same, she rather liked the air of confidence.

"An old professional family, even of that kind, must have gathered its traditions, Agatha," said S. of P.

"Fact is, Shelmerdine," said the Friend of the Family, "the young fellow has done a dashed sight better than anybody thinks he has—and a dashed sight better than he deserves, if you want my candid opinion."

Neither Father nor Mother appeared to want this candid opinion particularly, and yet they didn't appear very sorry to have it. And they went home feeling a little brighter for this interview; and, perhaps shaken a little in the Victorian Attitude. It was inconceivable that *She* would ever be able to do them credit; but might it not be that they had alarmed themselves a little unduly?

Still, it is easier, as a rule, to support the ills of others than to bear one's own. It was very well for Warlock to take this optimistic view; but Philip was not his son, and She was not his daughter-in-law. Nevertheless, they were glad, on the whole, that the wind had been tempered for them in this quarter. They didn't feel very forgiving just at present, though.

A little light was thrown upon the unlooked-for magnanimity of the Friend of the Family about a week later. For this the *Morning Post* was responsible, and the illumination was the following:—

"A marriage has been arranged and will shortly take place between the Marquis of Craigenputtock, eldest son of the Duke and Duchess of Dumbarton, and the Lady Adela Rocklaw, youngest daughter of the Earl of Warlock, K. C. M. G."

Everything for the best in the best of all possible worlds, you see. Father and Mother rejoiced, of course, at this cheering announcement; yet they did not seem exactly to overflow with joy when they called to convey their felicitations to dear Adela and her papa. But more than ever now were they inclined to doubt the *bona fides* of the latter in respect of the brave face he had put on their common misfortune.

Still, most warmly and affectionately did they congratulate Dumbarton's future duchess, whom they had the signal good fortune to find in black velvet with the Himalayan Dust Spaniel reclining at her feet.

The Happy Young Man, twenty-two years of age and rather fine drawn, was handing tea-cake. Pa had rather a twinkle in his eye—Pa had no right to let it be seen, though—when he presented the young fellow to Mother and Father; and Mother and Father congratulated him with the greatest warmth and spontaneity.

The felicitations were accepted of course in the spirit in which they were offered; and for our part we are very glad that dear Adela was able to let bygones be bygones, for, as all the world knew, Father and Mother had not been in the least to blame. Besides, it shows there was a core of magnanimity in the girl, and for this even we were hardly prepared, if we must confess the truth.

Pray do not think that Adela's good fortune was a mere figure of speech, since there was every reason to believe that the latest Scalp depending from the girdle of the Huntress was in all respects a very choice specimen. He looked one, certainly; and Mother, who was quite competent to form an opinion on such an abstruse subject, could tell by the way in which he handed hot buttered tea-cake that he had a beautiful nature.

Then Father had been at Eton with his father, and that, of course, was another point in the young man's favor.

"By the way," said the Ex-Ambassador, "I see in *The Thunderer* this morning that Philip is going into politics."

This was news for Father. Mother was incredulous.

"And as a Tag, Rag and Bobtail, if you please," said Pa quietly.

Father it was who was now smitten with incredulity.

"Impossible," he said.

Pa sent for *The Thunderer*, and there it was, as plain as your hand, that Mr. Philip Shelmerdine, the son of Lord Shelmerdine of Potterhanworth, had been adopted by the party of progress to fight their cause at Blackhampton.

"Boy must be insane," said Father. "He won't get in, at any rate—there's that consolation. I don't know any man more unfitted for public life."

"He may learn a wrinkle or two, though, Shelmerdine. A deuced clever wife he's married, you know."

"He'll need a clever wife if he is going to get in as a Rag at Blackhampton. It's—it's an act of insanity."

Then it was that Adela's young man made his *faux pas*.

"Married the celebrated actress, didn't he?" said Adela's young man.

The only thing to be said for him is that he was not at all well up in recent history.

Silence—complete and rather profound.

"I remember seeing her in a pantomime at Christmas, and I thought she was the jolliest girl I had ever seen—on the stage, I mean."

The afterthought sounded sincere; and the whole speech was animated by the best of intentions. But it really was not very clever of the young fellow. Yes, young fellow, this was a passage in which you did not shine particularly. Dumbarton's future duchess scowled at you—it would be idle to pretend that she didn't—Mother looked daggers; the great Proconsul's eyebrows said, "Shut up, you young fool," as audibly as eyebrows could indulge in that expression; and your future father-in-law had that satyr-like air which most people thought so damned unpleasant; but to you, young man, in your heedlessness, these signs and portents were without significance.

Your tenantry will doubtless keep always a warm corner for you in their hearts; and when you lead your charming bride to the altar you will be the recipient of a massive silver tea-service, no doubt; but if you continue in this way it is unlikely that posterity will be able to point out your effigy in marble, and in knee-breeches, too, to its great grandchildren as it walks along Whitehall. Yes, really a very tactless young fellow.

"Warlock," said Father bitterly, "I think that boy of mine must be mad. I wouldn't have had this happen for a very great deal. I don't know what Vandeleur will think, I'm sure."

"I can tell you, Shelmerdine," said the possessor of the satyr-like air, smiling grimly at the empty fireplace. "Vandeleur will think there is no tooth so keen as man's ingratitude."

"Warlock," said Father, with clenched hands, "it's damnable. And Vandeleur morbidly sensitive, too, on the question of personal loyalty. Can't we stop the young scoundrel?"

Warlock, speaking in mournful accents proper to a Constitutional crisis, failed to see how the young scoundrel could be stopped without invoking the aid of a commission in lunacy.

"Fellow's mad enough, Warlock, if it comes to that."

"Certainly, Shelmerdine, his latest action has all the appearance of insanity."

"This must go no farther, Warlock," said the imperious Ex-Resident of Barataria, North-West.

"I really hope it may not," said the Ex-Ambassador; "for the sake of you, for the sake of us, for the sake of Vandeleur, for the sake of the Empire."

A skeptical judgment might have doubted the sincerity of such a speech proceeding from such a quarter, but Father and Mother accepted it in simple good faith.

CHAPTER XXVI
A CONSTITUTIONAL CRISIS

WHY people should be so vexed by things that other people, equally serious of mind, don't care twopence about is one of the enigmas that is best left to the philosophers.

Father and Mother were much upset by Mr. Philip's act of treachery. Yet there was really no need for them to take it so tragically. The heir to the barony had attained the age when a man is allowed to do a little private thinking. But neither Father nor Mother was in sympathy with that point of view.

Something must be done in this national crisis. Energetic action must be taken. Mr. Vandeleur would never forgive it; the Party would never forgive it; the Country would never forgive it; the Empire would never forgive it.

If you make a practice of thinking imperially, you must view things on a comprehensive basis.

By the irony of circumstance, Mother and Father were dining out that evening in the Inner Circles of the Party. It was a small and quite unofficial occasion; but several of the Heads would be there.

"Agatha, it is the deuce," said the Proconsul, wrestling with his white tie.

"It is that Woman, I am convinced. Phil-ipp has been led on to this."

"I don't know what Vandeleur will say, I'm sure. And such a supercilious fellow when he gets really *cross*. Of course, I dissociate myself entirely from a step so subversive."

The Heads certainly received Father somewhat askance that evening. In parenthesis, it may be remarked that the world at large considered S. of P. as being by way of a Head himself. But things are not always what they seem, as Monsieur Bergson said of the Nebular Hypothesis. A Head he was, of course, in ordinary assembly; but this assembly, small though it was, was by no means ordinary.

It was the Hostess, a massive daughter of Caledonia, who first referred to the Vexed Subject, just as Father, with a rather poor appetite, had begun upon his bird.

"Lord Shelmerdine, what is this one hears about your son standing as a Rag?"

No; it was not exactly kind of Caledonia's daughter. The pause was awkward, particularly as Mr. Everard Vandeleur was seated on the right of his hostess.

"I have no need to say that I dissociate myself entirely from this ill-considered action," said S. of P. at length. "Beyond that I say nothing."

"But you must say something, Shelmerdine," thought the Front Bench, of which Two were present in addition to Mr. Everard Vandeleur. "It will create a most unhappy impression in the country."

"I can only attribute it to a mental aberration," said S. of P.

Mr. Everard Vandeleur shook his Jesuitical gray curls.

"Shelmerdine, my dear fellow," he said in tones vibrant with emotion, "I would rather have lost five seats in the country than this should have occurred."

"I had rather you had done so, Vandeleur, than that this should have taken place."

"Can you impose no check?" said Mr. Vandeleur. "Can you not refuse supply?"

"Unfortunately, no. The young scoundrel has a private income. But I hold his wife responsible for this."

"His wife?" said Mr. Vandeleur.

"The root of an evil," said the Husband of the Hostess, who, to be sure, was right at the other end of the mahogany.

"Your boy has married a wife, has he?" said Mr. Vandeleur, with the air of one who asks politely for information.

And who do you think, my lords and gentlemen, was seated opposite the Great Man? No less an individual than his Britannic Majesty's former Ambassador to Persia.

Not a living soul saw the glance that may or may not have passed between them.

"A great deal of marrying and giving in marriage these days, apparently," mused Mr. Everard Vandeleur.

"Your turn next, Van," said a Privileged Individual, whose brilliant sally, of course, set the table in a roar.

"Married a wife, has he?" mused Mr. Everard Vandeleur. "Good for the state, although not always good for the state of Denmark. And she has brought him to this. Well, well."

"It is revenge, of course," said S. of P.

A word so sinister caused the whole table to cock its ears.

"Revenge, Lord Shelmerdine!" said Caledonia's daughter.

"She is not received in the Family at present, and we get this stab in the back in consequence."

Two persons round the opposition mahogany were as grim as griffins. One was Father and the other was Mother. For the rest of the company it would be unsafe to answer.

"Why isn't she received in the Family?" said Caledonia's daughter, as blunt a woman as you would find in a long day's journey.

"He married contrary to the wishes of his parents," said Mother, preening her plumage at the hostess in a way which said quite clearly that she would thank her to be careful, as the ground was rather delicate. "Old-fashioned ideas, perhaps, but such marriages can only end in a general weakening of responsibility."

"I am out of my depth," said the plaintive Mr. Vandeleur. "But the position as I envisage it, is this: Your son's wife, out of favor at Court, plots against the dynasty. The dynasty trembles—"

"I beg your pardon, Mr. Vandeleur, it does nothing of the kind," said a very significant factor in the dynasty.

"Metaphorically, of course, Lady Shelmerdine. I speak in metaphor. The dynasty trembles because a bombshell has been thrown in the country—nothing less than a bombshell, as I unhesitatingly affirm—and to avert ruin one course only appears to be open to it."

"What is that course, Mr. Vandeleur?" said Lady Shelmerdine.

"To compose this internecine quarrel, and avert a further sanguinary conflict," said Mr. Vandeleur.

A great man had spoken. Consols fell habitually at his *Obiter Dicta*. French Rentes and Russia Fours lost a whole point when he tore up his card in a medal round. No wonder that his outline of Imperial policy received the most respectful attention.

"Let the Family receive her, and pray let us have no more of it," said Caledonia's blunt daughter.

A suggestion of a great man in the interests of international comity is one thing; but untimely interference from one who has no *locus standi* beyond the fact that she has three addresses and more diamonds than are good for her, is quite another. Mother's eyes sparkled with the light of battle.

"Will it *really* make any difference to the Party, Mr. Vandeleur, his standing for Blackhampton?"

"Bound to convey an unfortunate impression, Lady Shelmerdine."

"But he can't possibly get in."

"One is glad to know that. But, being the son of his father, think of the weight he will carry with the Rags!"

The compliment was a little double-edged, perhaps, to some minds, but happily only one aspect of it was visible except to the Cynical, with whom, of course, this narrative has nothing to do.

"Why can't he possibly get in?" inquired the Hostess.

"No brains," said Father.

"At least, not many," corrected Mother.

"All the more likely to be returned as a Rag by Blackhampton," said Caledonia's daughter. "Don't you think so, Mr. Vandeleur?"

Mr. Vandeleur being a wise statesman, and the question being rather technical, he ignored it blandly.

"Shelmerdine, I think you ought to realize that we can't have him standing for Blackhampton as a Rag in any case, when we have barely enough candidates of our own to go round."

"Yes, I do realize that, my dear Vandeleur. I realize it most fully. Steps shall be taken. Steps shall be taken at once."

"Receive the girl in the Family—a nice girl, too, I'm told—and let us hear no more of it," said the Hostess to Mother, who would not have been averse from striking her for her effrontery.

What a pity it is that diamonds in excess are so demoralizing.

Full and ample forgiveness on the part of Grosvenor Square seemed to be indicated, provided that a proper humility and a reversion to the *status quo ante* was forthcoming on the part of the erring. Let the young woman be received in the Family, provided that the heir to the barony withdrew his odious candidature for Blackhampton, had said in effect the Leader of the Opposition; and a tolerably easy constituency should be provided for the young man. He might then emerge as a full-blown Wagger after a period of grace in which to atone for his naughtiness.

Father and Mother drove home in the electric brougham pondering deeply the wisdom of the sage. It would mean a considerable sacrifice of personal dignity thus to bargain with Her. They were a little surprised and even a little grieved, perhaps, that the Great Man had shown so scant a consideration for their domestic feelings; but then it was a familiar trait of his that he was ever ready to sacrifice the individual upon the altar of Party.

It looked like Humble Pie, and patrician stomachs are not very fond of that dish. But there did not seem to be any way out of it. The ukase had gone forth from the Chief that this wicked and immoral candidature must not proceed. It was bound to create a most unfortunate impression in the country. It only remained for them, in the opinion of that wise and far-seeing statesman, to swallow the bitter portion and make peace on honorable terms.

"One thing, Agatha, we may congratulate ourselves upon, at any rate," said the Proconsul. "Vandeleur took it much better than we had reason to expect."

"That is very well, Wally. But don't let us congratulate ourselves too soon. It may not be so easy to get him to withdraw as Mr. Vandeleur supposes."

"But if we offer a clean slate?" said the Proconsul.

"When a man is clearly infatuated," said Mother, who was often inclined to sententiousness about this hour of the evening, "you can count on nothing beyond the fact that She will make herself as disagreeable as possible."

In what manner should the olive-branch be conveyed by the dove of peace? Delicacy was called for. Was Mother or was Father the better qualified to exercise it? Mother had not been altogether a success in the rôle of the diplomatist at large. It was idle to shut one's eyes to that fact, wasn't it? But then, had Father? Really, if it came to that, neither had much margin for self-congratulation. And when all is said, Humble Pie is not a very eupeptic form of diet.

"Wally," said the Colthurst of Suffolk at the breakfast table on the following morning, "I have given the matter most anxious consideration, and I think, having regard to everything, it is, perhaps, best left in my hands."

The Proconsul looked just a little dubious as he removed the top of a hard-boiled egg.

"You are quite sure, Agatha, that you feel competent?"

"*Quite*, Wally."

"Well, perhaps you are right. I hope so, at all events."

It was decided that Mother should call in Knightsbridge that afternoon upon Daughter-in-law, in spite of the Danger.

"That I will risk," said Mother, who at heart was an Amazon. "Only once have I seen her, and that was in Bedford Gardens, and she opened the door to me holding a potato in one hand and a knife in the other."

As the case had been represented to Father, he was quite prepared to believe even that.

"If you would like me to accompany you, Agatha," said the Proconsul gallantly, "I will cut the Select Committee this afternoon."

But Mother seemed to feel quite competent to take care of herself; and, after all, Father saw no real reason to doubt her ability.

Accordingly, at the punctual hour of half-past four that afternoon, Mother entered the lift at Park Mansions, and was hoisted in a patent elevator to the threshold of the Guilty Pair.

Happily, on this occasion her ring was answered not by a damsel, a knife and a potato, but by an undeniably smart young parlor-maid, who was quite trim enough to please the most severely critical.

Was Mrs. Shelmerdine at home?

The S. Y. P., who had charming natural manners, smiled a really very nice affirmative.

As Mother entered the domain of the Guilty Pair, it seemed to her that everything in the little vestibule, and there was hardly anything in it to speak of, was, considering all things, in surprisingly good taste.

"Why, Mater, this is awfully sweet of you," said the manly voice of Mr. Philip.

Salutations of a filial and unaffected character. The young man was really not deep enough to be wary. All was about to be forgiven, evidently, else the good old mater would not be calling upon 'em. Nevertheless, a little surprise was in store for this optimist. Mary, whose amiable custom it was to meet the whole world a little more than half way, did not exactly throw herself into the arms of Mother.

Mother, moreover, did not exactly cast herself upon the neck of Mary.

They chose to shake hands rather than have recourse to any less formal style of reception.

"So nice of you, Lady Shelmerdine, to find your way up to our little foot in the air."

It was said very cool and smiling, but if the young minx had left it unsaid it would have been just as well, perhaps, since somehow it didn't seem to help things particularly.

"The art furniture is more comfortable than it looks, Lady Shelmerdine," said the young Madam archly. "Try this one. Don't you like our yellow wall-paper? Phil-ipp's taste is so wonderful. Will you have some tea?"

Mother would be pleased to have some tea, but it was by no means clear, for all that, that Mrs. Philip was yet in the Family.

The young Madam poured out tea as though she didn't mind very much whether she was in the Family or whether she wasn't. Young ladies of Newnham and Girton, we can't help thinking, although it grieves us terribly to criticize the Heroine, that this was very wrong of her. Mother was eating Humble Pie, and she ought to have been trying a little as well.

The Twin Brethren handed the tea to Mother in quite their ablest manner.

"Have some muffin while it's warm, Mater."

Mother preferred bread and butter, thank you.

Conversation seemed to languish rather, until Mother made the important discovery that you got quite a nice view of the park.

"Toppin'!" said Mr. Philip.

"I'm afraid these flats must be dreadfully expensive," said the Maternal One.

"Not for the position, Mater."

Mother hoped not, at any rate.

"I hope you have noticed our Whistler, Lady Shelmerdine?" said Mary the demure.

Oh, *where* was the Whistler? Mother was *so* fond of canaries.

Calamity nearly overtook the muffin of Daughter-in-law. Happily it stopped at very nearly.

"The little picture opposite, Lady Shelmerdine. But you can't really see it now the sun has got round to the west."

Mother had to examine the gem, of course, like any other art critic. Glasses did great execution. Which was the Whistler? Ah, yes, to be sure, the name of the artist. An artist with a name so original was bound to be rated highly. A present from Sir Herbert Forrest, the famous actor-manager. Yes, Mother had seen him as the Woodman in *Twelfth Night*. How interesting to have such a memento from such a famous man. And how *well* you could see the park. And she did *hope* it was not too expensive. And everything in such *good* taste, although yellow for a wall-paper was a rather *modern* color. And such *delicious* tea. And what *charming* cups. A present from Mr. Vandeleur. How kind—a memento, of course, of his respect and admiration for dear Phil-ipp's father.

"It didn't say so on the card, though, Mater," said dear Phil-ipp with a clumsiness for which, perhaps, he is to be forgiven. "It said on the card, 'To Cinderella, from a Humble Admirer who wishes her every happiness.'"

So nice of Mr. Vandeleur to be so tactful. Could there be a clearer indication of Mr. Vandeleur's esteem for a friend and colleague?

It hadn't occurred to Hubby, though, that this really charming china tea-set was in any way connected with the great Proconsul.

Mother was a little hurt by this unfilial obtuseness. As though there could be any other reason. Mr. Vandeleur was so able, so responsible. However, the tea-service was charming—and blue china, too.

These were elegant preliminaries, but Mother's mission was both high and delicate. *Enormous* tact was needed, you know. *Suaviter in Modo* this time at least.

Was it correct that Philip was standing for Parliament?—Oh, yes.

But as a Rag, Tag, and Bobtail, according to *The Thunderer*?—Yes, the Leading Morning Journal was correctly informed.

Somehow that seemed merely to leave matters in a state of suspended animation. Philip was pleasantly frank, yet without being particularly communicative. Mrs. Philip seemed wholly absorbed in the vernal prospect.

"I am sure, dear Phil-ipp, you will be sorry to know that your father is upset."

Like a dutiful son, Phil-ipp was *awfully* sorry.

"And Mr. Vandeleur, of course. Your father was the last peer made by his Gover'ment. So wounding to a man as sensitive as Mr. Vandeleur!"

Mr. Philip was awfully sorry that his little adventure was being taken so seriously by people whom he would not have supposed would have paid it any attention.

"But, dear Phil-ipp," said Mother, "your father holds such a *special* position in public life. He is *so* upset. A real grief to him, with the affairs of the country in their present deplorable state. The Constitution, you know—! *Dear* Phil-ipp, have you fully considered the question?"

Oh, yes, dear Phil-ipp had considered the question—that is, as well as he was able to. He didn't pretend that he knew very much about it; but Polly rather thought—the prophetic soul of Mother!—but Polly rather thought that a man of means and leisure ought to go into Parliament, and try and make himself useful to the world. Not that personally he felt he would be of any use at all.

"I can only say, dear Phil-ipp," said Mother, "that your father is much upset; Mr. Vandeleur is much upset; the Party is much upset; and we have all talked about you quite anxiously. Don't you realize what an amount of political capital will be made of your standing as a Rag by the enemies of the Empire?"

"I shouldn't have thought anybody would have cared twopence about it, Mater. It isn't as though I had any ability."

"It is not *you*, of course, who matters so much. It is your dear father who carries so much weight in the country."

But Mr. Philip supposed, though not at all disrespectfully, that a chap of twenty-eight was entitled to have views of his own.

Mother didn't quite agree with that general proposition. There were some things, for instance, Religion and Politics to name only two, although there were others she could have mentioned, in which it was only right for a well-born and expensively nurtured Englishman to defer to the more matured wisdom of his ancestors.

Mr. Philip was awfully sorry, but he rather believed in Progress.

Mother was a little inclined to snort at Progress. What, pray, did one who had got as far as he had want with Progress! As far as Mother could see, the current idea of Progress was to take money out of the pockets of those who were better off than yourself, and put it into your own.

"And there is no reason for *you* to resort to that, Phil-ipp," said Mother, with a sudden effusion of Inspired Commonsense; "because you have more than the majority."

Daughter-in-law, still looking through the window, and wholly absorbed in contemplation of the vernal prospect, was suddenly overwhelmed by a dreadful fear lest the histrionic temperament, which was her own private and particular cross, should make an exhibition of itself.

Mother was fearfully good at argument, and always had been. Phil-ipp, of course, was the merest child at it, even though he had been selected by the Party of Progress to fight their great cause. Mother in her inmost heart thought it was the clearest proof of the contemptible level of Rag intellect, that any body of registered voters should have brought themselves to confide in any such candidate. And Mother nearly boiled over when Mr. Philip made an even more abject confession of his impotence.

"Come and argue with the Mater a bit," said he to fair Nature's admirer, still at gaze upon the vernal prospect. "She's much too clever for me."

Should Mother take off the gloves? No, decidedly more Politic not to remove them. Mother's third chin advanced a little, though, in spite of herself. This daughter of the people was likely to know more about the peeling of potatoes than of the conduct of high politics.

At the summons of her lord, however, the young minx controlled her mobile features as well as in her lay; and in that designing mind was the question, Should she toy a little with this Victorian Mamma? Or should she exercise her arts and blandishments?

"It is so wrong of Phil-ipp," said Mother, "and I think *you* ought to exercise the influence that every wife—that is, if she is good and worthy—has with her husband, and dissuade him from this course. You do see, do you not, that it is most injudicious for a man in his position?"

"Well, Lady Shelmerdine," said Mischief, having decided in favor of the broader way, "Phil-ipp looks at it like this—don't you, Phil-ipp? The Rags do get on a bit, but the Waggers are generally going backwards."

Followed an academic discussion of the Situation. A most immoral proceeding, Mother was bound to believe. Ingratitude could not further go than for the eldest son of the very last peer created by Mr. Vandeleur's Gover'ment to go over horse, foot and artillery, to the foe.

"To what extent ought a son to suffer for the indiscretion of his father?" inquired Mischief solemnly.

Mother begged pardon; she didn't understand. Daughter-in-law seemed unable to render the question any clearer.

At this point the Conference seemed to take a turn for the worse.

Did Mrs. Shelmerdine really suppose, said Mother in crystal tones, that young men in the position of her husband had no responsibilities to society?

Oh, yes, Mrs. Shelmerdine was quite sure they had, and that was why personally she was so glad he had decided to throw in his lot with the party of Progress.

Progress, said Mother—What, pray, is Progress?

The question was rather difficult for a young married woman to answer. But fortunately it appeared that Phil-ipp was not depending wholly upon dialectics in the coming battle.

"I am sorry to hear it," said Mother.

Yes, that was rather subtle for Mother.

"I suppose you feel, Lady Shelmerdine," said the young wife, "that if he depended entirely on his mental powers he would have no chance of getting in."

Mother ignored the question, perhaps a little pointedly.

Well, it seemed that Phil-ipp had several other strings to his bow.

Mother had implicit faith, however, in the essential good sense of her countrymen in the Midlands. They were such shrewd people in the Midlands; and Mother hoped and believed they would demand qualities more positive than those guaranteed by the fact that the Rag candidate was the eldest son of a distinguished father.

Mischief agreed; but if the Candidate was able to kick three goals against Aston Villa, which he was quite capable of doing if he went into special training for the purpose, in the opinion of the local experts, there was no power on earth that could keep him from the head of the poll.

This, of course, took Mother out of her depth completely. She herself was something of an old parliamentary hand; and she had gained first-hand experience in the days when the Proconsul was merely Sir Walter and a light of the House of Commons. But this was beyond her.

Mother had never heard of Aston Villa; and when Daughter-in-law took pains to explain who Aston Villa was, somehow Mother didn't seem much enlightened. But of one thing she was sure. To fight a parliamentary election upon any such basis was subversive of the Constitution.

No, somehow the Conference didn't seem to prosper. Nevertheless, Mother was there with the olive-branch; but really, in the circumstances, she didn't quite see what use could be made of the floral emblem. Still, an effort would have to be made.

To do justice to Mother, she was quite prepared to eat Humble Pie. It was most unlikely that any good would come of the act of deglutition; still, desperate remedies were called for.

"To be perfectly candid, Phil-ipp," said Mother, really getting to business at last, "your father has taken counsel of Mr. Vandeleur—most anxious counsel; and, acting upon his suggestion, he is fully prepared to offer a warm welcome to you both in Grosvenor Square; and he very much hopes you will allow your name to be withdrawn, and sometime, quite soon, Mr. Vandeleur himself will find you a constituency, because he is really concerned that a young man of such promise should be lost to the party."

Thus did Mother grapple right nobly with the unsavory cates. Perhaps her table manners were not quite so delicate as some people's might have been; but let none be so heartless as to criticize her when she is wrestling so nobly with her Cross.

Phil-ipp and Mary were touched, of course, by the liberal offer; touched very deeply, although they didn't quite see how it would be possible for the former to go back on his principles, even allowing for the fact that the fatted calf is such delectable fare. They were awfully nice about it, though, which is, of course, what you would expect them to be; very gentle and polite and even affectionate with Mother, who was doing her best in circumstances quite foreign to her nature.

All the same, the conclusion of the Conference was by no means all that could have been desired. The guilty pair had involved themselves so deeply with Blackhampton that they couldn't very well draw back. Besides, it was not wholly clear that they wanted to. After all, a man who had attained the ripe age of twenty-eight might aspire to a few convictions. Phil-ipp felt so strongly that the future lay with the party of Progress.

Mother failed undoubtedly in her diplomatic errand. And no doubt the measure of her failure was in her parting words that dear Phil-ipp would never be forgiven by his father if he persisted in going to the poll.

Mother took an affectionate leave of her peccant son, but her leave of Daughter-in-law was very guarded.

CHAPTER XXVII
ANOTHER TRIUMPH FOR FREE TRADE

THINGS had to go forward at Blackhampton in spite of the Ukase, and forward they went right merrily. The adoption of Philip was a fine stroke on the part of the Rags, because the Blackhampton Rovers had a following of about thirty thousand persons weekly, and one and all of these acclaimed it as quite the right policy. The famous inside right had had in his day—which was not so very far off either—only one superior in that responsible position, and he was Steve Bloomer. If the Rag candidate could only reproduce his form on a great occasion, he was bound to go straight to the top of the poll.

A general election was expected in the autumn. Philip and Mary spent August at Trouville in order to prepare for the fray. Philip trained on the sands, and Mary composed speeches while she listened to the seductive strains of Monsieur Marly's Marine Orchestra. And then, when this delightful month was over, they went to Blackhampton in fighting trim; hired a house for three months on its outskirts, and set to work in grim earnest.

In a very short time they were the two most popular people in this rather unalluring city. It was democratic to the core; and the fact that the Rag candidate was the son of Mr. Vandeleur's very last creation was made a cardinal point by his opponents. But, as the candidate said with simple pathos at every meeting—Gentlemen, it is not fair to hold me responsible for my father. No man ought to be held responsible for his father. I am doing my level best to live down my father, gentlemen, and in so doing I look confidently for the support of every follower of the Rovers in this room, for they, I know, are good sportsmen.

Whereupon the good sportsmen in question invariably roared themselves hoarse.

And then the Candidate would proceed: Gentlemen, I am not much use at a speech. But I'll just say this. I hope we shall beat the Villa on Saturday. (Uproar.) It won't be for want of trying, anyhow. (Uproar.) And if we do manage to beat 'em, and I think we shall—(cries of "Good lad!")—I hope you will be kind enough to forgive my oratory (cries of "Rather!" and loud cheering).

And now, gentlemen, I am going to ask my wife, who is a far better speaker than I am, to say a few words. There is no need for me to make you known to one another, because she tells me you are all old friends of hers. (Loud cheers, and cries of "Sing us a song, Mary!")

Mary, looking like a picture-postcard, would then sit down to the piano, which with great foresight had been provided by the Executive Committee, and proceed to sing that famous ballad from *Iolanthe* about good Queen Bess's glorious days when the House of Lords did nothing in particular, and did it very well. That was pretty well for a beginning; and the audience would be so delighted with this effort that she was not allowed to get to her speech until she had sung all the old favorites that had made her so famous. And then, when she had sung all her songs, the Chairman, Mr. Alderman Slocock, would interpose and say that it was really not fair to insist on her making a speech, because if they did she might have no voice left the following evening for the great meeting at the Corn Exchange. And this course having been commended by the meeting as a rare example of political foresight, the proceedings terminated with the usual vote of confidence, in which there was not a single dissentient voice.

Aston Villa were beaten handsomely on the following Saturday; and, although the Candidate only managed to kick one goal, he showed so much of his old form that it was clear already that another striking blow had been delivered against the House of Lords. In fact, that tottering institution had not a look in, really. Its meetings were very tame affairs by comparison, even if the standard of speech-making was thought by some people to be higher. But little or no interest was taken in them; while at those of the unfilial young man, who was going to take away his father's Veto, there wasn't even standing room an hour before the proceedings began.

Undoubtedly it was going to be a signal triumph for the People's Cause. The Candidate combined so well with the rest of the Rovers' forwards that the Wolverhampton Wanderers were beaten on their own ground, and Manchester City were simply annihilated. "Deeds not Words" flamed forth in the Rag colors, a vivid orange, from every hoarding. If the Candidate only kept up his form, said those who knew (and there was a surprising amount of omniscience in Blackhampton just now), the Rovers were bound to win the Cup and Mr. Balsquith would make him Home Secretary immediately.

In spite of all the adulation he received, the Candidate remained very simple and modest about it all. Even after he had scored two goals against Sheffield Wednesday, he never attempted any particular flight of oratory. The Missus could do all that so much better. No doubt she could have done, but South-West Blackhampton was far too wise in its day and generation to give her the chance. Let her attend to the piano. That, in the opinion of South-West Blackhampton, was so much more important.

The dissolution of Parliament occurred in the middle of November. A crowded and glorious fortnight followed. Notts Forest were beaten; a draw was made with Sunderland; and on the very eve of the poll Tottenham Hotspur received a most crushing reverse.

For the second time in its ignoble history, Protection was not only dead but damned.

It was all over bar the shouting, even before the fateful day had dawned. The Flag-Waggers could hardly raise a waggle; the sitting member realized already that he had lost his seat. Blackhampton went solidly for the Rags, and the best inside right in England—never mind Steve Bloomer!—was hoisted with a noble majority to the top of the poll.

Unparalleled scenes were enacted in Market Square. The horses were taken out of the New Member's carriage, and he and his charming wife were drawn in triumph through the principal streets.

A deputation with Alderman Slocock at its head waited on the New Member at his committee room the morning after the declaration of the poll. The Rovers hoped in all humility that their famous inside right would not desert them now.

Desert the Rovers! Nothing was further from the New Member's intention. Certainly he would play for them for the rest of the season if only they were good enough to choose him. And the deputation withdrew, after further congratulations upon his deserved success, and having further acclaimed him as a true sportsman.

Some members of Parliament might have been rather bored by having to play every week for the Blackhampton Rovers, but that was not the case with Philip. He had renewed his youth; never in his life had he more thoroughly enjoyed this manly game. Besides, he had all Blackhampton for his friends. He was a really great man in Blackhampton, and even self-effacing people like to know that places exist where their merits are appreciated.

Nevertheless, when the news reached Grosvenor Square that the Rags had gained a seat at Blackhampton, and that the turnover of votes had been tremendous, surprise was mingled with consternation.

"It wasn't as if the fellow had any brains," said Father to everybody.

Mother, however, informed the world privately that she always thought dear Phil-ipp had been underrated by his father. It was very wrong, of course, to stand as a Rag, but no young man wholly devoid of ability could possibly have gained a seat like South-West Blackhampton with such an enormous majority.

Still, Grosvenor Square was quite at a loss to understand it. But one thing was clear. The breach was widened by this painful incident; at least, Father, in his blindness, thought so. Had failure been the portion of this wicked revolt, forgiveness would have been easier. Its dazzling success seemed to put forgiveness out of the question.

Mother, perhaps, was inclined to weaken a bit. After all, did it really matter so much? And was it not better than leading an idle and useless life? However misplaced the ambition, surely it was an evidence of that dormant ability, which in her heart she had always known to be there, since her family was never without it.

Father, however, was adamant. It was an open flout. Moreover, it had rendered him ridiculous in the Inner Circle, which, however, so far from viewing the matter with exaggerated grief was rather inclined to see in it a joke of a high order. Why this should have been the case Father had no means of knowing. To one of his own staunch principles it was certainly no laughing matter.

As time passed, the maternal heart of Mother was disposed to relent, but Father, alas! would not hear of compromise. He felt too keenly this double act of filial disloyalty. It was rather absurd to view things in this light, said the friends of both parties, but the Proconsul was adamant.

He went his way, and Philip and Mary went theirs. In spite of their wrong-doing the guilty pair contrived to be extremely happy in the little nest at Knightsbridge. But Father, alas! grew exceedingly miserable.

Even Mother had come to agree with the world, that Father was not behaving with his usual wisdom. Mrs. Philip was really less Bohemian than Mother had feared, in spite of the incident of the potato. If she were duly encouraged, she might have the makings of a good wife.

Indeed, by the time the Guilty Pair had been married a little more than a year, Mrs. Philip certainly fulfilled one of the important duties incident to the degree in life to which it had pleased Providence to call her. As a matter of fact, she overdid it a little, in the opinion of persons qualified to speak with authority. She presented Philip with Twins.

Alas! even when the glad news was borne to Father, he remained firm in his attitude. He still played the part of Achilles sulking in his tent, although it was openly said by all right-minded people that such conduct was entirely unworthy of a great Proconsul.

One thing was clear, however, now that this joyful event had occurred. The little nest in Knightsbridge was no longer adequate. A move was therefore made to a more commodious abode in Pont Street.

Philip was almost ridiculously proud to be a father. He went up and down the metropolis in a way that must have been intolerable to those who do not love the human race. He had "had his leg pulled" pretty severely over his return for South-West Blackhampton, but that was nothing in comparison with what he had now to endure.

"What are you going to call 'em, Shel, old boy?" was the greeting of all and sundry.

Two lusty men they were, whose lungs thus early in life did infinite credit to both parents.

To the credit of Mother, be it said, the Twins proved altogether too much for her. She hauled down her flag completely, and even went to the length of consenting to meet the goddaughter of Edward Bean in consultation. There had been faults on both sides, perhaps. Still, the goddaughter of Edward Bean, whose eyesight, to be sure, was not what it used to be, was only able to see faults on one side.

Nevertheless, the lion lay down with the lamb; and Mother herself took charge of the removal to Pont Street. Moreover, she even went to the length of choosing a desirable residence; and insisted on furnishing it in part with a dole from the privy purse. Yet, while Mother was behaving in this rational and sensible manner and was thus laying up a store of happiness for herself, Father declined to be comforted, and every day made himself more unhappy.

Tragedy began to hover around the pillows of the great Proconsul. His appetite declined; his clothes no longer fitted him; no longer did he seem to care about public business as of yore. Instead of the succession being doubly secure, the Family might have been threatened with extinction.

CHAPTER XXVIII
THE END OF THE TALE

IT was Mary's custom to give the Twins an airing in the park every morning when the weather was fine. Like a wise young mother, she personally undertook this important duty; trundling the perambulator herself, and gaining health and happiness thereby, in spite of the emphatic protests of Philip, who seemed to think that nursemaids had been invented for that purpose.

This was a subject, however, upon which Mary was a little inclined to dogmatism. A mother who was young and strong, and as absurdly proud as she was of her progeny, should show herself to be worthy of the good gifts of heaven by taking a thoroughly practical interest in their welfare. This was pretty sound doctrine, the Member for Blackhampton was obliged to admit, although personally he rather thought that nursemaids—

Mary had no belief in nursemaids.

Thereupon the proud father, in spite of an involuntary shudder of the Twin Brethren—within his own breast, of course, not those within the vehicle—felt that he himself should be allowed to undertake this onerous duty.

Mary laughed at this. It was not the business of Man to push perambulators, and no self-respecting woman would ever endure the spectacle.

The pushing of the perambulator had all the elements of a pretty little quarrel in it; but these young married people were much too modern and sensible to conduct themselves in that old and foolish fashion. *Amantium iræ* amused them not. Real pals don't snarl at one another, whatever Q. Horatius may have to say upon the subject.

Therefore the proud father had to capitulate. Besides, said Mary, it would never do for white spats by Grant and Cockburn to condescend to such a menial occupation. The Button Club would certainly expel their wearer if he was guilty of any such solecism. Even as it was, rumor had it that he had been severely reprimanded by the Committee for daring to stand as a Rag for Blackhampton, and worse, of getting himself elected by a considerable majority. If he were to be seen pushing a "pram" in the park on a fine June morning, he would be compelled to resign his membership of the institution.

The member for Blackhampton had to yield; and Mary was left in undisputed possession of her perambulator and its lusty occupants. And certainly, as she trundled the vehicle along the railings of the Row, she looked just about the nicest and proudest and happiest young mother in the metropolis. It is true that on one occasion when the proud father was accompanying the procession *à cheval*, one of England's future duchesses gave the young mother and her perambulator a decidedly disdainful look as she passed them; and also that one of England's future dukes looked very hard at them, and, moreover, turned round to stare after them, which was hardly what you would expect, and we hope you will pardon his grossly unducal behavior. Still, the provocation was great. Here was one of the mothers of the nation to which we are all proud to belong, whether we are Rags or whether we are Waggers, a simple, sensible, square-browed young matron, a picture of well-being, who, having given two noble kids to the world, was determined to look after 'em.

The young woman with the perambulator made a fascinating picture on these fine June mornings, along by the railings of the Row; and had it been painted by Rembrandt or Velasquez or some other old and respectable painter, a good deal of money might have been offered for it by cosmopolitan millionaires.

Indeed, the Young Woman with the Perambulator became rather a source of remark for some of the *habitués* of the thoroughfare. Elderly gentlemen with well-brushed side-whiskers, grandfathers all, remarked upon her to other elderly gentlemen. Sensible girl, they said, doing good to herself and to the nation at large, and setting an example to others. It was far better than leaving 'em to nursemaids and suchlike careless hussies. You *know* that they are all right when you have charge of them yourself.

It chanced one morning as the procession followed its accustomed course, with Philip near at hand, mounted on a quadruped that had turned out better as a hack than as a 'chaser, a distinguished personage came upon the scene in faultless morning attire. He was none other than Arminius Wingrove.

A man of such wisdom could not do less than stay to admire the Twins. For the life of him, though, he couldn't say which side of the family they favored most. Walter Augustus, named after the misguided Grandpapa who had declined to attend the christening, had certainly the eyes of his mother; Philip Archibald had certainly the eyes of his mother also. The nose of Philip Archibald was, undoubtedly, that of his father; the nose of Walter Augustus was undoubtedly that of his father also; while as for the mouth, the mouth of both Walter Augustus and Philip Archibald was undoubtedly that of both parents. Still, it must not be thought that Walter

Augustus and Philip Archibald had always to endure those imposing names. One was called Bow and the other was called Wow in domestic circles.

So unfeigned was the admiration of Arminius Wingrove that nothing would content him but that he should turn and accompany the procession as far as the Achilles statue. But before they were able to gain that desirable bourn, which itself commemorates a great moment in the life of the nation, yet one more historic incident was destined to occur. Alas, that its only commemoration is like to be these unworthy pages!

However, if the Board of Supererogation, evidences of whose romantic disposition are to be found all over our fair metropolis, really feels disposed to mark the precise spot where this historic episode came to pass, it may be said that it was exactly opposite the little kiosk for the sale of newspapers and other undesirable forms of literature which has been permitted to invade the chaste precincts of what was once considered the most exclusive spot in all London.

An elderly gentleman in a glossy silk hat, with well-brushed eyebrows and of a mien of generally composed importance, was debouching slowly yet all unknown into this historic episode. He was not looking very happy for all that he wore his habitual air of distinction. He was a Proconsul, and full many of the passers-by saluted him respectfully. But he did not seem in anywise the better for these manifestations of public regard.

If the truth must be told of this elderly gentleman, sorrow and envy were the occupants of his heart this lovely June morning, when even the metropolitan prospect was all that was fair and gracious. He was the most miserable grandfather in London, instead of being the proudest and happiest, as he certainly ought to have been.

In his stately progress he passed other grandfathers. They were walking with their sons and daughters, and with the sons and daughters of their sons and daughters, and looking immeasurably the better for the privilege. Surely, it was good to be a grandfather on this fine June morning. It seemed a perfectly honorable and rational and proper state of being.

Every yard he walked, the conviction grew firmer in him that this was the case. It was surely the duty of elderly gentlemen with well-brushed eyebrows to rejoice in that degree. There was a man he knew well, a member of Parliament, looking so pink and prosperous, with a small girl holding one hand and a small boy holding the other. Envy and sorrow were not in that heart, it was certain.

Could it be that his recent policy had been vain and weak and shortsighted? The great Proconsul had never asked himself such questions before, but it was becoming increasingly clear to him that he would have to be asking them presently. A grandfather had surely no right to make himself as ridiculous as he had done.

Then it was that the great Proconsul came right opposite the Achilles statue, and the episode to which we have already referred got itself made into history. A certain Mr. Wingrove, a famous dramatist who had been elected recently under the rule *honoris causâ* to Grandfather's club, and with whom Grandfather was upon pleasantly familiar terms, came into view. Walking by the side of Mr. Wingrove was a charming-looking girl. She had charge of a most commodious double perambulator, and so proudly was she trundling it that it was quite clear to the acute perception of the great Proconsul that this was a case of Twins.

Grandfather, in his present somewhat emotional state, must needs stop and shake Mr. Wingrove heartily by the hand. And, further, he was constrained to offer his sincere congratulations. He overflowed with admiration.

"And *what* are their names?" he asked.

"One is called Bow, and the other is called Wow," said the demure young mother.

It seemed passing strange to Mr. Wingrove that the great Proconsul should not know the names of his own grandchildren, and, moreover, that he should not recognize them and their mother. Then a light dawned suddenly upon him. Further, it seemed to this sagacious mind that in the absence of the lawful father, who had turned his horse and who was going now down the Row at a canter, that a legitimate opportunity had presented itself for the exercise of the comic spirit.

"I should really like my wife to see them," said the great Proconsul. "Such splendid fellows; the picture of health."

"Oh, yes, by all means," said Mr. Wingrove, with a rather sly smile at the proud young mother.

No time like the present. If Mrs. W. didn't mind bringing along these infant phenomena as far as Grosvenor Square, which is hardly ten minutes' walk from the Achilles statue as the crow flies, he was sure that Lady S. would be enchanted.

The gracious young matron would be delighted to take them round to Grosvenor Square for the inspection of the wife of this most agreeable elderly gentleman, whose name, by the way, she had not the pleasure of knowing. All the same, the mention of Grosvenor Square and the demeanor of Mr. Wingrove combined to give the young madam a pretty shrewd suspicion.

As for Arminius Wingrove, he was amazed at the resource and the boldness of Providence, which, of course, he was quite entitled to be. And in that, to be sure, he was by no means singular. Many first-rate minds have been similarly occupied for some little time past.

Grandfather, all unconscious of the wicked trick that Fate had put upon him, prattled along by the side of the four-wheeled chariot; and he was presently moved to indulge in the proud confidence that they had recently had Twins in the Family.

"Oh, really," said Mr. Wingrove.

"Oh, how interesting," said the proud young mother, not to be outdone in gravity.

"I must really go and see 'em," said Grandfather.

"Oh, haven't you seen them yet?" said the fair charioteer.

Not yet. It seemed that a Proconsul had so many calls upon his attention.

"Well, if I was their mother, I don't think I should be very pleased with *you*. Haven't you been rather remiss, Mr.—? I haven't the pleasure of knowing your name."

"Lord Shelmerdine," said Mr. Wingrove, hastening to atone for his sin of omission.

By this, they were waiting to cross Park Lane.

"Shall I tell him yours?" whispered the famous playwright to Mrs. Philip.

"No, of course you mustn't," said that designing young Madam. "Unless you want to spoil everything."

THE END